A GHOSTLY
GOOD TIME

Woman's Day. Special Interest Publications

A GHOSTLY GOOD TIME

The Family Halloween Handbook

filipacchi
publishing

Copyright © 2008 Filipacchi Publishing, a division of Hachette Filipacchi Media U.S., Inc.

First published in 2008 in the United States of America by

Filipacchi Publishing
1633 Broadway
New York, NY 10019

Woman's Day Special Interest Publications is a registered trademark of Hachette Filipacchi Media U.S., Inc.

DESIGN: Patricia Fabricant
COPYEDITING: Jennifer Ladonne
PRODUCTION: Ed Barredo

ISBN 10: 1-933231-46-7
ISBN 13: 978-1-933231-46-4

Library of Congress Control Number: 2008924230

Printed in China

CONTENTS

CHAPTER 1
HALLOWEEN HEADQUARTERS:
Outdoor and Indoor Decorations

6

CHAPTER 2
DRESSED TO THRILL:
Costumes for the Whole Family

50

CHAPTER 3
LITTLE WORKSHOP OF HORRORS:
Creepy Crafts

72

CHAPTER 4
DEVILISH DELIGHTS:
Snacks and Treats

94

CREDITS
128

HALLOWEEN HEADQUARTERS: OUTDOOR AND INDOOR DECORATIONS

Halloween curb appeal translates into all things fun and frightful. Thrill neighborhood revelers with a hair-raising outdoor decor; and cast a spell over your home with decorating projects that are easy and creative. Whether you're aiming for something silly for the kids or sophisticated for friends and neighbors, these charming ideas are positively bewitching.

Ghostly Estate Herald this special season with a pageant of decorations. Foam-board gravestones painted gray, along with fake bones and skulls from the craft store, brew up a haunting mood. Add a big chain in front for rattling and it's "Run for your life, everybody!"

EERIE EXTERIORS
Outdoor decors

A bounty of jack-o'-lanterns, ghostly spiderwebs and a grisly graveyard will have trick-or-treaters of all ages quaking and shaking happily in their shoes.

Paper Witches

SKILL LEVEL: Beginner

MATERIALS: Tracing paper; pencil; transfer paper; roll of kraft paper; scissors; clear double-stick tape.

DIRECTIONS:

1 Enlarge Paper Witches patterns, below (see *How to Enlarge Patterns*, page 128). Trace patterns onto tracing paper. Using transfer paper, transfer outlines onto kraft paper; cut out.

2 Using tape, adhere witches in windows.

Skull Luminarias

SKILL LEVEL: Beginner

MATERIALS: Tracing paper; pencil; transfer paper; black construction paper; cutting mat; craft knife; glue stick; white paper lunch bags; sand; votive candles in glasses.
NOTE: Do not allow candles to burn unattended.

DIRECTIONS:

1 Enlarge Skull Luminaria pattern, right (see *How to Enlarge Patterns*, page 128). Trace pattern onto tracing paper. Using transfer paper, transfer outlines onto black paper.

2 Place paper on cutting mat. Using craft knife, cut out pattern, cutting away lighter sections of pattern.

one square = 1 inch

3 Rub back of pattern with glue stick; press onto front of bag.

4 Fill bag with several inches of sand. Place votive in center of sand.

one square = 1 inch

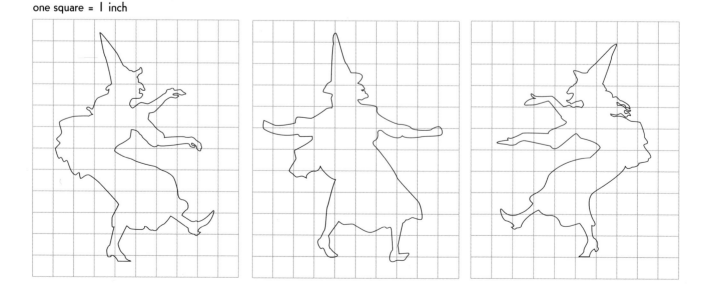

Paper Witches flying across well-
lit windows lend a haunting bit of
mischief. Light the path to your door
with Skull Luminarias. Print templates
out on white bags using the envelope
setting on your computer printer or
cut patterns out of black craft paper
and glue them on the bags.

Hand Cutouts

SKILL LEVEL: Intermediate (parents should help kids)

MATERIALS: Large pumpkins; large serrated knife; pumpkin cleaning kit (scoop and small knife); black spray paint; scissors; masking tape; chalk marking pencil; votive candles.

NOTE: Do not allow candles to burn unattended.

DIRECTIONS:

1 Using serrated knife, cut tops off pumpkins by cutting in circle around stem. Lift out and reserve.

2 Scoop out seeds and pulp, leaving at least a 1-inch shell.

3 Replace tops on pumpkins; apply several light, even coats of paint to entire pumpkin, letting dry after each coat.

4 Enlarge hand cutout patterns, right (see *How to Enlarge Patterns*, page 128). Cut out patterns.

5 Tape patterns to pumpkins; using chalk pencil, draw around outlines.

6 Using knife from pumpkin cleaning kit, cut out hand shapes along outlines. Remove cutouts from pumpkin.

7 Place votive candle inside pumpkin; light candle and replace top.

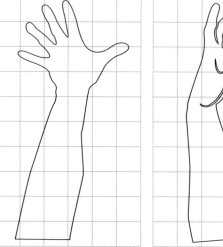
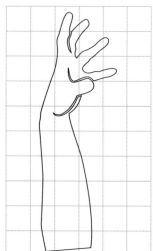
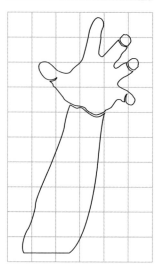

one square = 1 inch

Spooktacular Welcome

SKILL LEVEL: Beginner

SIZE: About 5 feet high

MATERIALS: Newspaper; masking tape; pencil; galvanized wire: 5 yards of 12-gauge, 3 yards of 14-gauge; pliers; 8-inch-square of copper roof flashing; heavy-duty scissors or metal shears; hammer and nail; 1 yard of tie wire; string of small white Christmas lights (about 130 lights); electrician's tape; spool of clear fishing line.

DIRECTIONS:

1 Tape sheets of newspaper together to form one sheet about 5 x 3-feet for a pattern. Draw ghost pattern on paper, making ghost about 5 feet high and about 3 feet wide at arms.

2 Starting at bottom point of ghost, bend 12-gauge wire to follow pattern. Use pliers for tight curves and corners. Weight wire down as you bend it to help keep shape.

3 Bend each end into hook; hook ends together and tighten with pliers.

4 For supports, attach pieces of 14-gauge wire across ghost frame from side to side in several spots. Attach two supports, 3 inches apart, across head for eye support.

5 Make an 2½ x 4½ oval newspaper pattern for eyes. Using pattern, cut two eyes from copper flashing.

6 Tape eyes to wood scraps or pile of old magazines, then use hammer and nail to punch large hole in center of each eye. Hole should be large enough to insert Christmas light. Also punch 2 holes on each side of eye, making holes 3 inches apart for support. Hammer each eye lightly in center so eyes cup inward.

7 Attach eyes to support wires on frame with small pieces of tie wire.

8 Starting at bottom point of ghost, wind lights around frame up to lower eye support wire. Using electrician's tape, tape lights along support wire, inserting a bulb through each eyehole, then tape lights back along same support wire and continue wrapping frame, ending at bottom point.

This Spooktacular Welcome is made using a galvanized wire frame and little white lights, with copper sheet metal to outline the blinking eyes. This ghost can be mounted onto a wall, a large tree or a porch. He's guaranteed to dazzle visitors and passersby alike.

9 If lights along eye support wire can be removed without causing the entire string to fail, remove those bulbs; if not, place electrician's tape over them.

10 Use fishing line to hang ghost; also tie fishing line to a weight at bottom of ghost to keep it stable.

▼ **Lofty Visions** Who-o-o-o goes there in the shadows? A fake feathered or plastic owl perching on your lamppost will give trick-or-treaters a friendly scare. Festoon the post with ghostly spider webbing to make it even eerier. Special effects like a flickering light bulb and a recording of a hooting owl thicken the plot.

▲ **Eye See You** A string of plastic monster lights twinkling amid the branches could be visitors from outer space or fierce animals on the prowl. One thing's for sure, visitors won't want to get close enough to investigate. You can reuse this sort of outdoor decoration for years to come.

◀ **Step Up** Arrange a memorable vignette: a medley of lit pumpkins, one feisty cat howling hello, two ravens and a sprinkling of teeny white lights. A lone tree silhouette in the window is all it takes to conjure up thoughts of gloomy forests and glens.

▶ **Scared Silly** Abracadabra! Turn an old suit into a gruesome headless presence. Pin one arm across the front to form a resting spot for a grinning faux pumpkin. Black gloves, black shoes and a colorful bandanna are perfect underworld accessories. Should Mr. Creepy need a companion, only a supersize spider will do.

◀ **Special Delivery** This mailbox garden goblin doesn't miss a thing. Fake flower stems hold his horrific craft-store-foam eyes aloft amid a swirl of pretend vines. A gaping red mouth and white teeth cut from craft foam glued to the mailbox's front imbue the creepy critter with a particularly hungry expression.

▶ **Cut Ups** This snowman-like sculpture is simply three pumpkins stacked in graduated sizes. Turn the top pumpkin on its side to use the stem as a nose, then carve a whimsical face or draw one on with black marker. Stick arms, a basket hat and a Halloween sign complete the picture with jolly flair.

PUMPKIN PRIMER
Jaunty Jack-O'-Lanterns
Usher in the Holiday

Nothing symbolizes Halloween like pumpkins sporting a spooky face and a flickering candle. Named for a character in Irish folklore called Jack, who tried too hard to outwit the devil, jack-o'-lanterns today can be big or small, carved or painted, scary or silly—but always fun for kids and grownups alike.

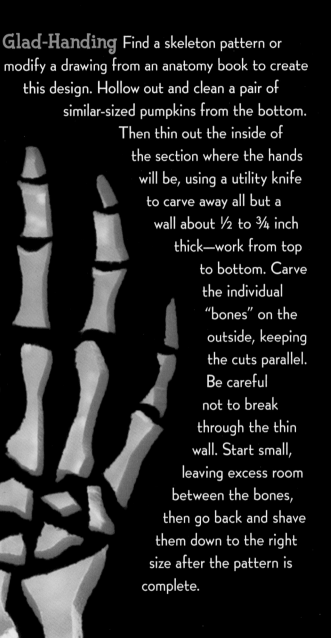

Glad-Handing Find a skeleton pattern or modify a drawing from an anatomy book to create this design. Hollow out and clean a pair of similar-sized pumpkins from the bottom. Then thin out the inside of the section where the hands will be, using a utility knife to carve away all but a wall about ½ to ¾ inch thick—work from top to bottom. Carve the individual "bones" on the outside, keeping the cuts parallel. Be careful not to break through the thin wall. Start small, leaving excess room between the bones, then go back and shave them down to the right size after the pattern is complete.

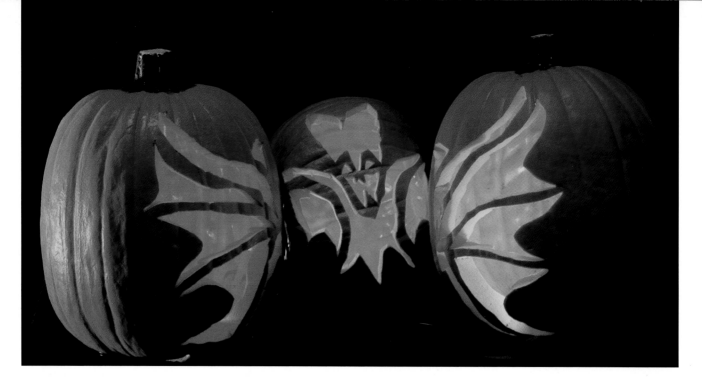

▲Going Bats You'll need three pretty pumpkins for this project: two matching ones for the wings, and a smaller one for the body. (Place all three together before you buy them to make sure they'll look good together.) Empty them of seeds through the bottom. Sketch the body on the small pumpkin. The trickiest part is orienting the wings so they match up with the body. Draw a wing on paper and etch it into one of the large pumpkins with a sharpened pencil or awl. Flip the wing over and transfer the mirror image to the other large pumpkin. Double-check the alignment, then get carving!

▼ Creepy, Crawly Spiders The designs for these realistic-looking arachnids were adapted from an entomology textbook—if you're not up to triplets, make just one pattern and orient it in three different directions. When planning a spider carving, imagine it wrapping itself around the pumpkin. Sketch, then carve very carefully, keeping the cuts parallel and headed into the center of the pumpkin to avoid accidentally removing more than the design requires; space out the legs to give yourself extra margin for error.

Friendly Feline This grinning Cheshire cat is a snap to make—once you find the purrfect pumpkin! As with all these pumpkin designs, access is through the bottom. First, sketch kitty freehand on the face of your hollowed-out canvas, then use a utility knife to cut out the design, starting with the nose and working your way out. Be extra careful with the delicate curving lines of the eyebrows and whiskers. Then light a candle and get ready for smiles all around at this cat's meow.

▲ **Portraits on a Pumpkin** Ask your kids to make some funny faces, then snap a few digital photos. Choose the pics you like best for inspiration—if you have a printer, you can even blow them up larger to serve as a pattern. Exaggerate the features with your pencil for comic or spooky effect, translating eyes, mouth and nose into bold cutouts for carving. Fine details, like the eyebrows and tears on the middle pumpkin, can be created by using a sharp pencil, or an awl or ice pick to punch holes through the outside.

◀ **Eye Spy** Take a close look at your eyes in the mirror, or find a good picture of eyes. Clean out your pumpkin (from the bottom), then sketch the design on the skin. The secret to a perfect pupil? Start your work with an apple corer, carving your way out from the center. Poke the pieces out from the inside, especially with tricky areas like the eyebrows, so as not to damage the delicate design.

Hey, Bonehead! When you're done with this skull, you'll have the best jack-o'-lantern on the block. Start with a freehand drawing or a pattern, and transfer it to the face of a cleaned pumpkin. Cut out the general design first; you'll refine it later. Start with the center—in this case, the nose—and work outward. Create the suggestion of a skull with partial cuts that keep the pumpkin intact at the top. When you're ready to carve the mouth, start with the general shape, then go back in and finish the details.

Pumpkin Pointers

What would Halloween be without a few pumpkins to carve? Here are some basic tips:

1 Look for pumpkins with flat bottoms, smooth contours and well-shaped, healthy-looking stems.

2 Scrub pumpkin with soap and water to remove dirt and any exterior residue, then allow it to dry thoroughly.

3 Assemble all the tools ahead of time, including newspapers or a plastic tarp for protecting work surfaces; a bowl for collecting seeds; and knives and spoons. Some carvers use a keyhole saw for cutting through the skin.

4 If your pumpkin won't stand up straight, cut a thin slice from the bottom to provide a stable base and make the pumpkin easier to carve.

5 When cutting the lid, insert the knife at a slight angle, so the outside of the lid is a little bigger than the inside; this will keep the lid fitting snugly, instead of falling into the pumpkin.

6 Use a big spoon or ladle to clean out the seeds, scraping the inside rind until it's about an inch thick.

7 Leave space between features when cutting; if the openings are too close, the wall of the pumpkin might collapse.

8 To keep carved pumpkins from wrinkling as long as possible, coat cut surfaces with a thin layer of vegetable oil or petroleum jelly, which helps them retain moisture.

9 Display indoor pumpkins on a pretty tray, cake stand or even a piece of wood.

10 If you have any carved pumpkins that still look fresh after Halloween is over, keep them to use as impromptu seasonal vases for cut flowers or branches.

ROOMS WITH A BOO
Wickedly Fun Decorating Projects

ENTRYWAY & PORCH

A standard doormat becomes a tongue-in-cheek Un-Welcome Mat with a little spray paint. Don't forget to put it away after Halloween!

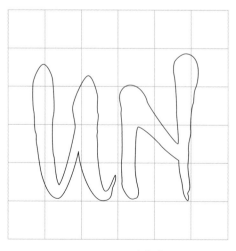

one square = 1 inch

Un-Welcome Mat

SKILL LEVEL: Beginner

MATERIALS: Stencil plastic; fine-point black permanent marker; craft knife; cutting mat; stencil adhesive; purchased welcome mat; red outdoor spray paint.

DIRECTIONS:

1 Enlarge Un-Welcome Mat pattern, below left (see *How to Enlarge Patterns*, page 128). Place stencil plastic over pattern; trace outlines with marker.

2 Place plastic on cutting mat and cut out stencil along marked lines.

3 Spray back of stencil with adhesive; place on mat in front of the word "welcome."

4 Apply several light coats of paint to stencil, working from edges to center and letting dry after each coat to prevent paint from seeping under stencil edges. Remove stencil; let dry.

Spider Wreath

SKILL LEVEL: Beginner

MATERIALS: Black spray paint; plastic foam wreath form in desired size; 2 feet of black 20-gauge wire; heavy-duty scissors; bag of black plastic spider rings (from party-favor or crafts store); hot-glue gun and glue sticks; silver glitter spray paint; ½ yard of 2-inch-wide black ribbon.

DIRECTIONS:

1 Paint wreath black; let dry.

2 Fold wire in half; twist along length. Fold in half again; twist ends together to form hanging loop. Twist ends of loop around top of wreath so loop extends at top.

3 Cut ring portions off spider rings. Glue spider portions to cover wreath completely.

4 Lightly spray wreath with glitter paint; let dry.

5 Tie ribbon in bow around side of wreath; trim ribbon ends diagonally.

Frightful Foyer Use your imagination to decorate the front hall, where guests will get a dazzling first impression. Stuffed owls and ravens, magic broomsticks and rubber mice are specialty-store collectibles you can use every year. Crafty projects include dried shrunken-head apples packed into an attractive glass jar, and a spooky Spider Wreath made from plastic spiders glued onto a plastic foam form painted black.

▶ Enter if You Dare An array of props, costumes and other fun stuff from party shops and specialty catalogs—hats, capes, brooms, and assorted scary gewgaws—sets the front-porch stage for all your festivities. Raid the closets and the attic to see what you can find!

◀ Phantom Operations
No haunted house would be complete without a fake severed arm! Purchase one at a local party store and pair it with the appropriate grisly tools of the trade, à la *Texas Chainsaw Massacre*. A vase of dead flowers enhances the fright factor.

▶ Look at the Birdie An antique black birdcage becomes the final resting place for a plastic or painted-wood bird skeleton model. Or, find a faux-feathered friend in a craft store and hang him upside-down from the perch.

LIVING ROOM

Window Treatments

SKILL LEVEL: Beginner

MATERIALS: Curtain rods and mounting hardware; tape measure; light- and medium-weight 90-inch-wide cheesecloth (available by the yard at fabric stores); scissors; large bucket; strong brewed tea; pins; sewing machine and thread.

DIRECTIONS:

1 Mount curtain rods in window frames.

2 Measure desired length of curtain; add 8 inches. Cut a piece of medium-weight cheesecloth to this length for each window.

3 Pour tea into bucket; submerge drapes in tea and allow to soak for several hours. Rinse well and allow to dry.

4 Turn under 8 inches on upper edge of each drape and pin in place; stitch 6 inches below fold to form pocket for curtain rod. Leave raw edges to shred for extra spookiness.

5 Slip rod through pocket and mount in window.

6 For valance, measure window width; cut lightweight cheesecloth into pieces 3 times as long as window width.

7 Drape valance loosely over rod to resemble spiderwebs.

Channel your inner interior decorator to create gruesome but graceful Window Treatments using two kinds of cheesecloth: heavy-weight for "drapes" that are tea-dyed for a musty look, and light-weight white for the wispy "valances" on top. Feel free to add ravens and bats, giant spiders, rubber snakes and furry stuffed hands from the party store, along with plenty of gourds, pumpkins and candles.

Make a festive forest with these whimsical Trick-or-Treat Trees, made from candy corn, peanut chews and Tootsie Rolls hot-glued onto plastic foam forms. Spray unwrapped sweets with sealant to keep them in place (heavier candies may require pins). Make sure little goblins know these are for looking at, not eating!

Trick-or-Treat Trees

SKILL LEVEL: Beginner

MATERIALS: Spray paints: black, orange; terra-cotta dish; plastic foam cone or tree form; small and medium plastic foam pumpkins; craft knife; skewer; 18-inch dowel; hot-glue gun and glue sticks; assorted candies (we used candy corn, wrapped peanut chews and wrapped Tootsie Rolls); T-pins; glitter spray (optional); spray polyurethane sealer (optional).
NOTE: Candy used on trees is not edible!

DIRECTIONS:

1 Paint dish and cone black; paint pumpkins orange. Let all pieces dry.

2 Using tip of knife, start hole in center bottom of cone. Push skewer into hole, then through center of cone as far as possible; this forms starter hole for dowel. Form hole at center top of cone in same manner so holes meet. Push dowel through hole so it extends evenly at each end.

3 Make hole through center of each pumpkin in same manner.

4 Push pumpkins onto dowel ends.

5 Starting at lower edge of cone, glue candies in rings around cone as you work toward top. For larger candies, use T-pins if needed.

6 Lightly spray pumpkins with glitter, if desired.

7 If using unwrapped candy, spray tree with sealer; let dry.

Fright Site Cut-out letters from an old magazine, gourds and cute hanging craft-store spiders on the mirror make an excellent view with a boo. Black spray-painted silk vines combined with folded-leaf moths create an eerie effect. For a finishing touch, add a few ghostly hands.

one square = 1 inch

Your couch will never be the same when you adorn it with Colorful Cushions created by using no-sew pillow covers. Guests will delight in the frightful jack-o'-lantern and haunting hoot owl patterns.

Colorful Cushions

SKILL LEVEL: Beginner

MATERIALS (for each pillow): Pencil; ½ yard of Heat n' Bond paper-backed fusible web; scissors; felt (for Pumpkin Pillow: 38-inch-square black, 16-inch-square orange, white and black remnants; for Hoot Owl Pillow: 38-inch-square orange, 16-inch-square black, white and orange remnants); iron; 16-inch piece of Velcro brand Fabric Fusion no-sew tape; 18-inch-square pillow form.

DIRECTIONS:

1 Enlarge Pumpkin Pillow pattern or Hoot Owl Pillow pattern, opposite (see *How to Enlarge Patterns*, page 128). Trace main pattern and all features onto Heat n' Bond; cut out, leaving ½-inch margin around each piece.

2 For Pumpkin, main pattern onto orange felt with iron, eyes and teeth onto white felt and inner eyes and nose onto black felt; cut out. For Hoot Owl, fuse pattern onto black felt, eyes onto white felt and nose and feet onto orange felt; cut out.

3 Peel off paper backing and arrange main pattern on center of large felt square. Fuse in place. Arrange and fuse all features on main square.

4 Cut Velcro into two equal pieces; separate sections. Fuse hook sections to upper and left side edges on right side of cover. Fuse loop sections to lower and right side edges on wrong side of cover.

5 Place cover face down; place pillow form in center. Overlap side edges of cover; press Velcro strips together. Fold upper and lower edges to center; fold back under layers to press Velcro strips together. Tuck in fabric edges.

Crackers

SKILL LEVEL: Beginner

MATERIALS: Crepe paper; ruler; scissors; tubes from toilet tissue rolls; clear double-stick tape or glue stick; roll of curling ribbon; small candies or party favors; decorative printed paper (such as origami paper or gift wrap).

DIRECTIONS:

1 Cut crepe paper into 8 x 10-inch pieces.

2 Roll paper lengthwise around tube so it extends evenly at both ends; tape or glue along length of tube.

3 Gather paper at one end of tube. Tie ribbon around gathers.

4 Fill tube with candy and favors; tie other end.

5 Cut decorative paper into 4 x 7-inch pieces. Wrap and glue paper around tube.

6 Using scissors, curl ribbon ends.

These nonexplosive Crackers are made from toilet tissue rolls and colorful crepe paper. Fill with candy and other goodies, then cover the telltale roll with printed craft paper for the perfect party memento. (You could also write guests' names on plain craft paper and use the poppers as place cards.)

DINING ROOM

◀ **Mirror, Mirror...** Create a ghostly message with this easy project. Tear letters out of newspaper; lay them on the mirror with light double-sided tape. Spray the surface with a matte finish spray. Allow to dry completely, then remove the letters (a razor blade helps with this). When all is said and done, use glass cleaner to restore the mirror.

Skeleton Garland

SKILL LEVEL: Beginner

MATERIALS: 27 x 20-inch sheet of medium-weight white paper; ruler; scissors; craft knife; cutting mat; iron; clear cellophane tape; glitter: orange, green; package of white Velcro Sticky Back coins.

DIRECTIONS:

1 Cut paper lengthwise into 5¾ x 20-inch strips.

2 Fold each strip accordion-style along its length, making folds 2½ inches apart.

3 Enlarge Skeleton Garland pattern, below (see *How to Enlarge Patterns*, page 128). Cut out pattern.

4 Place pattern on folded paper strip, placing center line of pattern on fold. Trace outline; cut out, forming garland (end skull will be half-skull).

5 Place garland on cutting mat. Using craft knife, cut out openings as marked on pattern.

6 Open out garland. Cut away half-skull, leaving 1-inch-long tab. Cut away other end of garland even with end of skull.

7 Using warm iron, press garland to remove fold lines.

8 Place strips of tape behind openings on skulls. Sprinkle glitter onto tape; shake off excess.

9 Attach Velcro coins to each tab to join strips. Also attach coins at ends of garland. Attach coins to wall to hang garland.

Bewitching Pictures

Print out animal templates in black, then cover already framed artwork with white paper, and affix the critters to the paper with double-sided tape. Make borders with hand-ripped black paper strips. Remove white paper after the festivities.

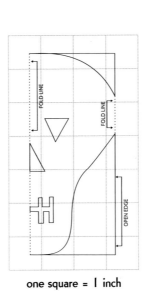

one square = 1 inch

The silly Skeleton Garland is made in sections and can be easily stored for next year. The bony noggins are cut from white paper folded accordion style, then cut. The more you make, the longer the garland gets.

Beaded Spiders

SKILL LEVEL: Intermediate

MATERIALS: Spool of 34-gauge wire; wire cutters; ruler; black seed beads; long black bugle beads; two 4mm black pearl beads; 6mm black pearl bead; 10mm "dazzleberry" bead (bead covered with woven seed beads to resemble raspberries); 2-inch head pin; wire cutters; needle-nose pliers.

DIRECTIONS:

1 Cut 30 inches of wire. Following bead-stringing diagram (below), string black bugle beads, alternating with black seed beads, pushing wire back up through each six beads as you go. Repeat 8 times to form all legs, leaving about 1 inch of wire between tops of legs.

2 Twist wire ends together to form ring. Twist center of ring and arrange legs with half on each side of center twist.

3 To make spider head and body, place 4mm bead, then 6mm bead, then 10mm berry bead, then 4mm bead, on head pin. Snip wire ½ inch past last bead; using pliers, bend small loop in wire for hanging.

4 With pliers, twist center of leg wire around head/body pin, just below berry bead, to join legs to head and body.

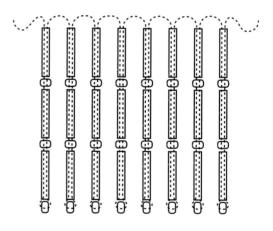

Clever Beaded Spiders made of wire and assorted beads do double-duty, spinning their way down from the chandelier, and perched on orange linen napkins courtesy of some narrow black ribbon.

Utensil Holders

SKILL LEVEL: Beginner

MATERIALS: 7-inch beige Velcro sew-on tape; black tracing paper; chalk pencil; sheets of craft foam or felt; craft glue; remnants of felt, feathers and other decorations as desired; glitter glue pen.

DIRECTIONS:

1 Enlarge Utensil Holder pattern, below (see *How to Enlarge Patterns*, page 128). Cut brim once and hat twice from foam or felt.

2 Glue hat sections together along sides, leaving upper straight edge open.

3 Cut out center of brim, as marked on pattern.

4 Glue center of brim to edges of hat, forming pocket.

5 Decorate as desired, using felt to make stars, hatband or other shapes as desired. Glue shapes and feathers in place.

6 If desired, add motifs with glitter glue pen.

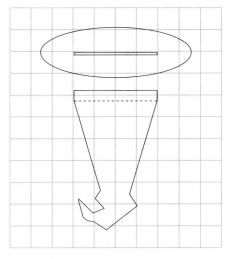

one square = 1 inch

Felt and feathers are transformed into festive Utensil Holders in a witch-hat shape made from a template. Trim with stars and brightly colored hatbands. The only tricky part is aligning the two parts of the hat to create the pocket.

Closet Caper Guests will scream with delight when they open a closet door and get a ghoulish greeting from a grinning grim reaper. To make, buy a skeleton and hang him from the closet's door frame so he pops out when the door is opened.

Cheesecloth Curtains

SKILL LEVEL: Beginner

MATERIALS: Cheesecloth (we used 2-yard packages from cooking-supply stores); scissors; double-sided tape or thumbtacks.

DIRECTIONS:

1 Cut cheesecloth longer and wider than window as desired. Tape or tack cheesecloth to top of inner window frame so excess drapes at middle, sides and bottom as desired.

2 Cut another piece of cheesecloth approximately same size as first. Tear holes and rip spots in cheesecloth, using scissors to start holes, if needed.

3 Drape and tape or tack cheesecloth over first layer, forming soft drapes.

Cheesecloth Curtains create the perfect backdrop for the classic dead-body-in-the-parlor scare tactic. Wrap a willing friend in an old dress and gauze and have the dearly departed sit up and return from the hereafter. Guests will freak!

Witch Canister Cover

SKILL LEVEL: Beginner

MATERIALS: Can or canister for base; tape measure; chalk marking pencil; scissors; felt: ½ yard purple, ⅜ yard black, remnants of orange, white and green; Fabri-tac by Beacon fabric glue; 7-inch piece of Velcro brand Fabric Fusion no-sew tape; iron; pins; pencil; ⅛ yard Heat n' Bond paper-backed fusible web; 2 small black flat-back beads; pipe cleaners: 3 black, 2 purple; pinking shears; large black pom-pom; 2 small google eyes; 8 x 20-inch piece of tulle; 6 inches of floral wire.

DIRECTIONS:

1 Measure canister height; add 1 inch. Measure around canister; add 1½ inches. Mark and cut purple felt to these measurements for cover.

2 Turn under ½ inch on upper and lower edges; glue.

3 Separate Velcro sections. With iron, fuse one section to right side of cover, centering it along one raw edge. Pin other section to wrong side of cover, centering it along other raw edge. Wrap cover around canister to check fit; adjust pins as needed and mark placement. Remove pins and fuse in place.

4 Enlarge Witch Canister Cover Face pattern, below, right (see *How to Enlarge Patterns*, page 128). Trace mouth pattern once, tooth pattern once and eye pattern twice onto Heat n' Bond; cut out, leaving ½-inch margin around each piece. Fuse mouth onto black felt, tooth onto white felt and eyes onto orange felt; cut out. Peel off paper backing and arrange features on center front of cover. Fuse in place.

5 Glue beads in centers of eyes.

6 Enlarge Witch Canister Cover Hat pattern, below, left (see *How to Enlarge Patterns*, page 128).

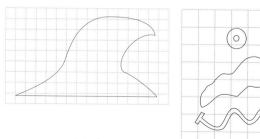

one square = 1 inch

The Witch Canister Cover, Cat Canister Cover and Skeleton Apron will come in mighty handy and get everyone into the holiday spirit.

Cut hat from black felt. On back of hat, glue one black pipe cleaner vertically and two pipe cleaners along lower edge to help keep its shape.

7 To make hair, use pinking shears to cut two 4-inch squares of green felt. Starting at one edge, make cuts every ¾ inch, stopping ½ inch from top. Glue hair sections under hat brim, spacing them about 3 inches apart.

8 To make spider, cut purple pipe cleaners in half. Twist the 4 pieces together once in center, then glue to back of pom-pom for legs. Bend into shape. Glue google eyes to front of pom-pom.

9 Gather up center of tulle along length; wrap center with wire to form 8-inch bow. Glue to underside of spider. Glue spider to hat.

10 Wrap and secure cover around canister. Glue lower edge of hat to cover at center so ends of hat extend past cover.

Cat Canister Cover

SKILL LEVEL: Beginner

MATERIALS: Can or canister for base; tape measure; chalk marking pencil; scissors; felt: ⅜ yard black, remnants of green, purple and orange; Fabri-tac by Beacon fabric glue; 7-inch piece of Velcro brand Fabric Fusion no-sew tape; iron; pins; pencil; remnant of Heat n' Bond paper-backed fusible web; 2 purple flat-back gems; 2 white pipe cleaners.

DIRECTIONS:

1 Measure canister height; add 1 inch. Measure around canister; add 1½ inches. Mark and cut purple felt to these measurements for cover.

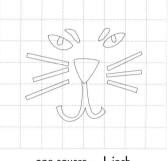

one square = 1 inch

2 Turn under ½ inch on upper and lower edges; glue.

3 Separate Velcro sections. Fuse one section to right side of cover, centering it along one raw edge. Pin other section to wrong side of cover, centering it along other raw edge. Wrap cover around canister to check fit; adjust pins as needed and mark placement. Remove pins and fuse in place with iron.

4 Enlarge Cat Canister Cover pattern, above (see *How to Enlarge Patterns*, page 128). Trace mouth pattern once, nose pattern once, eye pattern twice and inner-ear pattern twice onto Heat n' Bond; cut out, leaving ½-inch margin around each piece. Fuse mouth onto orange felt, nose and inner ears onto purple felt and eyes onto green felt; cut out. Peel off paper backing and arrange eyes, nose and mouth on center front of cover. Fuse in place.

5 Using outer-ear pattern, cut 2 outer ears from black felt. Peel off paper backing and fuse an inner ear onto each outer ear.

6 Glue gems in centers of eyes.

7 Cut six 2- to 3-inch whiskers from pipe cleaners; glue 3 whiskers on each side of nose.

8 Glue ears under upper edge of cover, spacing them about 3 inches apart.

9 Wrap and secure cover around canister.

Skeleton Apron

SKILL LEVEL: Beginner

MATERIALS: Felt: ¼ yard white, remnants of purple, orange, black; pencil; ¼ yard Heat n' Bond paper-backed fusible web; scissors; iron; 18-inch piece of Velcro brand Fabric Fusion no-sew tape; black cotton apron; Fabri-tac by Beacon fabric glue; 2 medium google eyes; 9 x 6-inch remnant of checked cotton fabric.
NOTE: Remove appliqué before washing apron.

DIRECTIONS:

1 Enlarge Skeleton Apron pattern, below (see *How to Enlarge Patterns*, page 128). Trace hat sections and facial features onto Heat n' Bond; cut out, leaving ½-inch margin around each piece. From white felt, cut entire head, including hat, for base.

2 Fuse hat band and cheeks onto orange felt, upper and lower hat onto purple felt and eyes, brows, nose and mouth onto black felt; cut out. Peel off paper backing and arrange hat and face on base. Fuse in place.

3 Cut Velcro into two equal pieces; separate sections. Fuse loop sections to back of base, near sides. Place base as desired on center front of apron; mark Velcro placement. Fuse hook sections to apron where marked.

4 Glue google eyes to centers of felt eyes.

5 Cut 1 x 6-inch strip of cotton fabric from one edge for knot (remaining fabric will be bow). Turn under ¼ inch on all edges of both fabric pieces; glue edges to hem.

6 Hand-gather center of bow fabric; wrap knot around center and glue. Trim excess knot fabric. Glue bow to skeleton's chin.

one square = 1 inch

BATHROOM

Hand Soap

SKILL LEVEL: Beginner

MATERIALS: Rubber craft hand or fingers; craft knife; soap-making kit (available at crafts store; includes materials and molds for microwave use) for clear glycerin soap.

DIRECTIONS:

1 Cut hand or fingers into pieces small enough to fit in soap molds.

2 Following manufacturer's directions, mix soap.

3 Pour soap to fill molds halfway. Place hand

or finger parts into molds, embedding them at least partially in soap. Allow to set for about 15 minutes.

4 Pour additional soap to top of each mold; allow to set according to kit directions.

5 Release soap from mold.

All Washed Up Give new meaning to "clean" with this carefully constructed powder-room frightscape, where you can let your imagination run wild. A standard soap-making kit and a few faux fingers from the party store are all it takes to create startlingly funny Hand Soap. Put a little playfulness in the old oral-hygiene routine: Hot-glue a set of fake choppers to the bottom of an old cotton-ball jar and fill with water, then fill a lab beaker with bright blue mouthwash. Recycle an old pill box as a nest for all sorts of creepy crawlies. Place sharp objects like an awl, rasp and green spray-painted wire scrub brush in the water glass. And don't forget the fake eyeballs and a few giant plastic cockroaches.

UP CLOSE & SCARY

▲ **Turn Out the Lights** On the mantel, arrange a spooky collection of crazy candlesticks, including a grinning skull and a raven that looks like it's straight out of Edgar Allen Poe—but really comes from a specialty catalog. Spray paint a wooden candlestick black to complete the terrifying tableau.

▲ **Make a List, Check it Twice** Even witches need a to-do list when they're conjuring up a celebration. Create yours on the computer, print it out and lightly spray paint the paper light brown. Burn the edges and you're done!

▶ **Not the Same Old Haunts** A collection of tin houses, purchased at yard sales, flea markets or party stores, transforms a windowsill or table into a street of screams. Backlight it with glimmering votive candles, and you'll be way ahead of the Joneses.

DRESSED TO THRILL: COSTUMES FOR THE WHOLE FAMILY

What's Halloween without a great costume? Grownups and kids alike will make a fiendishly fanciful appearance in these clever costumes. With just a few basic supermarket supplies and a little imagination you can terrify friends and neighbors, who'll wonder, "Who is this new ghoul on the block"?

Witch (for instructions, turn to page 52)

Three-Headed, Four-Armed Monster

SKILL LEVEL: Beginner

MATERIALS: Knee-high stockings; polyester fiberfill stuffing; 2 rubber full-head masks; 3 black knit ski caps; hot-glue gun; needle and thread; scissors; 2 red sweatshirts; 2 pairs of blue knit gloves; red sweatpants; safety pins; bandanna (optional).

DIRECTIONS:

1 Stuff stockings with fiberfill; tie ends. Stuff a stocking into each mask to form monster heads.

2 Glue a cap onto each head (child will wear remaining cap).

3 Hand-stitch a monster head to each side of child's cap.

4 Cut arms off one sweatshirt. Glue wrist ends shut. Stuff arms with fiberfill; glue upper ends shut to make fake arms.

5 Stuff 2 gloves with fiberfill; glue over wrist ends of fake arms.

6 Sew fake arms to sides of remaining sweatshirt, under sleeves.

7 Dress child in sweatshirt, sweatpants and remaining gloves. Place middle cap on child's head; safety pin fake heads to shoulders of sweatshirt. If using, tie bandanna around neck.

Wizard

SKILL LEVEL: Beginner

MATERIALS: Maroon pillowcase and queen-size sheet; scissors; chalk marking pencil; hot-glue gun; 4 yards of black felt; ruler; silver fabric paint pen; package of cheesecloth; black fabric dye; mixing bucket; 5-foot-long stick; plastic skull; rubber snake; sweat suit; 3 yards rope; face paint and fake beard.

DIRECTIONS:

1 Fold sheet in half crosswise; cut hole in center of fold large enough to place over head. Put sheet on.

2 Mark curved neckline on sheet, curving line down from back of neck to lower front edge of sheet. At about wrist level, mark cutting line, tapering down at an angle to several inches above ground. Mark back length of sheet several inches above ground.

3 Remove sheet. Cut along marked lines to form cape.

4 Cut two 2 x 20-inch ties from excess sheet; glue to front neckline on each side.

5 Cut felt into 3-inch-wide strips; glue to all edges of cape.

6 Cut two lightning-bolt shapes from black felt; glue to arm area of cape.

7 To make hood, cut along one side seam of pillowcase from hem edge to point, cutting in a curve.

8 About 6 inches from hem edge, cut a row of small holes 2 inches apart for drawstring, starting and ending 3 inches from cut edge. Cut a 1 x 30-inch strip from excess sheet; thread in and out of holes.

9 Glue felt strips to all edges of hood.

10 Using paint pen, draw designs on felt trim and lightning bolts on cape and hood.

11 Dye cheesecloth black; let dry. Cut into strips and pull threads to shred edges. Drape cheesecloth over stick. Glue skull to top; wrap and glue snake around lower portion of stick.

12 Dress in sweat suit; tie rope around waist. Place cape and hood on. Paint face and apply beard as desired.

Swamp Girl

Continue the flow of costume colors right onto the face in blocks: Apply a light pink powder base, then blend in accents of darker turquoise, jade green and eggplant purple eyeshadow. Make decorative petals with a lipliner brush and purple lipstick; use the same color on lips. To highlight, add deeper pink blush between mouth and chin and on the tip of the nose.

Swamp Girl

SKILL LEVEL: Beginner

MATERIALS: 10 yards of cheese-cloth; tie-dye pajamas; 3 colors dye in blue, teal and green; needle and thread; 2 bags assorted plastic bugs; hot-glue gun; headband.

DIRECTIONS:

1 Break cheesecloth into three groups; dye cheesecloth in three colors. Pull cheesecloth apart into thin strips and cut into assorted lengths. Lay the cheesecloth out across the pajama's arms, shoulders, neck and pants' waist, and using a needle, baste the cheesecloth to hang from the pajamas. Make layers. Shred cheesecloth with scissors. Attach plastic bugs with hot-glue gun.

2 To make headpiece, baste extra dyed-cheesecloth pieces to a headband.

Swamp Girl to Witch

SKILL LEVEL: Beginner

MATERIALS: Fabric dye: purple, emerald green, dark blue; large aluminum pans; bag of cheesecloth; plastic garbage bags; rubber gloves; 1 yard black burlap fabric; hot-glue gun; witch hat; striped stockings; black plastic crow.

DIRECTIONS:

1 Mix each color of dye in a separate pan, following dye directions.

2 Cover work area with plastic bags; wear gloves. Dip sections of old Swamp Girl costume into colors of dyes as desired. Divide cheesecloth into three parts; add one to each color of dye.

3 Rinse costume and cloth until water runs clear; dry.

4 To make skirt, cut burlap to desired skirt length. Cut lower edge into points. From remaining fabric, cut 4-inch-wide strip along length for waistband. Glue pleats along upper edge of skirt fabric, then glue pleated edge of skirt to waistband strip. Machine-wash and dry skirt so edges fray.

5 Dress child in costume, then in skirt. Glue additional layers of dyed cheesecloth to costume as desired.

Bat Boy

SKILL LEVEL: Beginner

MATERIALS: Tape measure; newspaper; scissors; pencil; 2 yards of green felt; ½ yard purple felt; hot-glue gun; 1 large bottle glitter paint; 2 yards of black, sticky-back hook-and-loop tape; poster board; blue plaid pajamas.

DIRECTIONS:

1 For wings, measure length of child's arm from neck to wrist; make a pattern for wings this length out of newspaper so you can test it for size. Then, using pattern and green felt, cut out wings with scalloped edges. Make sure the backside is longer than the front so when the wing drapes over the arm the backside will drop longer than the front.

2 Cut diamonds out of purple felt and glue to wings. Use glitter paint to edge the wings.

3 Use hook-and-loop tape to attach wings to arms. Cut it to length of pajama shirt from shoulder to wrist and attach. Attach other side of hook-and-loop tape to inside of wing as you want it to outline on child's arm.

4 Measure circumference of child's head. Cut a 1-inch-wide headband out of green felt with two ears as points on sides. To close, attach hook-and-loop tape to back.

5 Cut two matching ears for either side of head from purple felt, and two more ear patterns from thin cardboard. Place a cardboard ear on top of the ear on the headband, then a felt ear. Glue layers together using hot-glue gun.

Bat Boy

This makeup detail couldn't be simpler. With blue eyeliner pencil to match the costume's blue plaid pajamas, outline a bat shape with large outspread wings. Fill in with green powdered eyeshadow to complement the bat boy's green bat headgear with pointy green and purple ears.

Bat Boy to Dragon

SKILL LEVEL: Intermediate

MATERIALS: Felt: ½ yard *each* green, dark green, medium green and purple, 2 yards bright lime green; scissors; hot-glue gun; green knit hood or balaclava; 1 yard green ribbon; about 5 large rubber bands; black sweat suit; self-adhesive hook-and-loop tape; large safety pin.

DIRECTIONS:

1 Cut ½-yard pieces of felt into diamond shapes for dragon's scales. Remove wings from old Bat Boy costume; glue diamonds onto wings in overlapping layers, starting at lower edge. From lime green felt, cut a vest shape to fit front of sweatshirt. Glue in place. Glue additional felt triangles at bottom of vest.

2 Cut through chin portion of hood; turn under edges and glue. Cut ribbon into two equal lengths; glue at neck edge of hood for tie.

3 From dark green felt, cut ten 5½-inch-tall triangles for head spikes. Glue each pair of triangles together along 2 sides, leaving bottom open. Stuff lightly with felt scraps so spikes will stand up. Glue points down back of hood.

4 Determine desired length of tail. From medium green felt, cut a quarter-circle to this length.

5 Starting at wide end, roll tail felt into tight cone; secure with rubber bands at top and bottom, then add 2 or 3 more rubber bands at equal distances along tail. From all colors of felt, cut triangles in assorted sizes for scales. Glue scales to tail and sweatshirt.

6 Apply hook-and-loop tape to sweatshirt sleeves as in original Bat Boy costume; attach wings.

7 Using safety pin, attach tail to lower back of sweatshirt.

Garden Fairy

SKILL LEVEL: Intermediate

MATERIALS: Three 29 x 17-inch sheets of iridescent clear wrapping paper; ¾-inch clear adhesive tape; one ¼ x 36-inch ribbon; newspaper; scissors; 5 plastic foam sheets (3 dark pink, 2 light pink); headband; glue; 2 packages tissue paper, lavender and aqua; 2 packages green glitter pipe cleaners; 1 package white iridescent pipe cleaners; Flower-patterned pajama bottoms; aqua tank top; safety pin.

DIRECTIONS:

1 For skirt, take sheets of iridescent wrap. Lay flat on table lengthwise end to end, one sheet at a time. With your hands, starting at paper's side edge, gather in bunches taping just below top edge to hold and create a gathered waistband. Continue adding more paper until you have a skirt the circumference of child's waist. Lay ribbon over taped waist leaving ends to tie on both sides. Tape ribbon in place. Cut the bottom edge to desired length with a zigzag pattern.

2 Headband: make a pattern out of newspaper for 6-inch-long flower petals with a 2 x 1-inch tab on the end of each petal. Cut 9 petals from plastic foam sheets. Overlapping petals, wrap tabs tightly around headband and glue to back.

3 For tissue-paper flowers, cut a 10 x 12-inch square of tissue paper. Fold it in half 4 times until you have a 2-inch square. Pinch the bottom closed corner and twist, securing with a green pipe cleaner. Scallop cut the outer edges of the square and then open up petals to make a flower. Make enough to fill headband (about seven). Glue flowers to headband and wrap green pipe cleaners around headband making tendrils. For vine, twist multiple green pipe cleaners together. Add small tendrils extending from main vine and tissue paper flowers.

4 Make wings by cinching a sheet of iridescent gift wrap in the middle with a white iridescent pipe cleaner like a bow. Twist 3 white iridescent pipe cleaners into corkscrew shape; add to both sides for 3-D effect. Attach wings with safety pin.

Sponge on light blue and lavender eye shadow on forehead, adding tiny lavender flowers with green eyeliner centers. On sides, apply light red blush and create green eyeliner "vines" with eyeliner pencil to echo the costume's garden theme. Use blue-green shadow on eyelids, hot-pink lipstick on lips and a press-on jewel on forehead.

Garden Fairy to Clown

SKILL LEVEL: Intermediate

MATERIALS: Tissue paper: purple, pink, blue, patterned; scissors; ruler; roll of florist's tape; hot-glue gun; 2 yards of 2-inch-wide patterned ribbon; 5 large safety pins; green pipe cleaner; striped shirt and slippers.

DIRECTIONS:

1 Remove green vine pipe cleaners from Garden Fairy skirt.

2 Make at least 20 tissue-paper flowers for skirt as follows: For each flower, cut a 10-inch square of tissue paper from each color; layer papers and fold in quarters. Twist tape around folded corner. Cut scallops on outer edge; open out petals.

3 Glue paper flowers to skirt.

4 Cut Garden Fairy pajama pants to just below knee length. Cut ribbon into two equal lengths; pin one end of each piece to front of pants for suspenders. For bow, cut a 10" square of patterned tissue paper. Fold accordion style. Wrap green pipe cleaner around middle; fan out paper. Pin to shirt.

5 Dress child in shirt and pants; cross ribbon ends and pin to back of pants.

6 Remove large pink flower petals from Garden Fairy headband.

Spider

Rub deep red powder blush all over the face, extending out to the ears. On cheeks, draw a spider and web design with black eyeliner. Extend design up to forehead and down to chin. Use white eyeliner pencil sparingly to embellish the web, add depth to the spider body and create the spider's eyes.

Spider

SKILL LEVEL: Beginner

MATERIALS: Black pajamas (you can substitute thermals); small bath mat with rubber backing; scissors; 4 swimming pool noodles; twelve 6-inch lengths of pipe cleaners; eight 3- or 4-inch plastic food lids; hot-glue gun; glue sticks.

DIRECTIONS:

1 Fold mat in half (or cut a rectangle to width of shoulder); cut up back and make a neck hole in the center so that the mat goes over child's shoulders.

2 Cut noodles in half; slice ⅞ of the way though each tube in two places so tube bends downward, creating three segments for the spider legs. Reinforce connection of segments by sticking 6-inch pipe cleaners into ends of the tube foam.

3 Cut four holes in the mat on both sides where legs should be, making them the same size as the tube. Push an end of the noodle through the hole. Cut eight circles from plastic food lids slightly larger than hole.

4 Glue the circles to ends of the tubes, securing them to the mat surface.

Spider to Octopus

SKILL LEVEL: Intermediate

MATERIALS: Blue sweat suit; 1-inch flat paintbrush; acrylic paints: dark blue, light blue; ruler; craft knife; fine-point permanent black marker; scissors; two 24 x 15-inch rolls of bubble wrap; rubber bands; sheet of news-paper; pencil; hot-glue gun; large google eyes.

DIRECTIONS:

1 Paint dark and light-blue waves on sweat suit; let dry. Using craft knife, cut two 3-inch slices of noodle from old Spider legs, cutting a piece from a leg on each side of costume to keep legs even. Reserve pieces for hood.

2 Measure, mark and cut two 15 x 24-inch pieces of bubble wrap for each leg. Starting at top of each old Spider leg, roll a piece of bubble wrap loosely around noodle and secure with rubber bands at top, middle and bottom. Wrap and secure another

piece of wrap around lower edge of old leg so wrap extends 8 inches below end of noodle. Cover other legs in same manner.

3 Referring to photo, create head by drawing a helmet pattern on newspaper, making it tall and rounded at top and tapering slightly at bottom. Cut a hole near bottom of pattern for face. Hold pattern up to child's face to test size and placement of hole.

4 Using marker, trace pattern onto two sheets of bubble wrap; cut out.

5 Glue sides and top of head together, leaving bottom open.

6 Glue google eyes to ends of reserved noodle pieces. Glue eyes to headpiece, just above face hole. Fill top of head with crumpled remnants of bubble wrap to keep it round. Hot-glue sides together, leaving bottom open.

Star Man

SKILL LEVEL: Intermediate

MATERIALS: Space-themed pajamas; party store plastic construction helmet and sunglasses; silver spray paint; white glue; 1-inch plastic foam balls; 3 small bottles assorted glitter colors; assorted colors of pipe cleaners; hot-glue gun; scissors; 1 sheet *each* blue, red and yellow plastic foam sheets; silver-glitter paint pen; large black garbage bag; ½ x 36-inch black ribbon; 2-inch red, yellow and black duct tape; foil; sticky back hook-and-loop squares; metal repair tape; 5 reflective numbers or letters.

DIRECTIONS:

1 For helmet, spray paint child's plastic helmet with silver paint. Brush white glue over 1-inch plastic foam balls and roll in glitter to create planets. Dry. Push pipe cleaners into planets. Hot-glue to helmet. Cut yellow and red foam into stars; hot-glue to helmet. Hot-glue fun foam shapes to sides of sunglasses. Use silver-glitter paint pen to add squiggles on helmet.

2 For cape, cut top and one side of garbage bag open so it lies flat. Cut to desired length. Cut ½-inch slits across top of cape every 2 inches, approximately 1 inch down from top edge. Weave ribbon through slits and pull to gather to correct size. Cut width if cape is too wide. Use black duct tape to secure ribbon at neck edge.

3 For vest, measure length of child from shoulder to hip. Double this length. Lay four pieces of foil of this measurement on top of each other. Fold over in half and cut neck hole in center; cut up middle of one side for the back opening. Attach sticky back hook-and-loop squares to neck for closure. Cut up on a diagonal from bottom middle to the shoulders so that the vest tapers slightly from the shoulder to the waist. Edge all four vest layers with metal repair tape. Decorate the front of the vest with reflective numbers or letters and duct tape cut into various shapes.

Star Man

Start with a base of shiny silver eyeshadow for this intergalactic traveler. With an old blush brush, paint on thick, bright blue and yellow eye shadow stripes to pick up the colors and shapes in the sunglasses, foil shield and starry helmet. You may want to purchase some inexpensive cosmetic water-based face paint for the stripes.

Star Man to Robot

SKILL LEVEL: Intermediate

MATERIALS: Aluminum cookie sheet; small aluminum broiler pan; white or gray sweat suit; heavy-duty scissors; silver electrical tape; sheets of medium-weight aluminum ducting or flashing; aluminum pie plate; plastic cups; oven thermometer; black duct tape.

DIRECTIONS:

1 Tape cookie sheet and broiler pan to Star Man aluminum vest with silver tape. Dress child in sweat suit. Cut aluminum ducting to fit around arms and legs; secure in place with silver tape.

2 Using black tape, write number at bottom of pie plate; tape to bottom of vest with silver tape.

3 Carefully remove stars and balls from Star Man helmet; cover helmet completely with silver tape.

4 Using silver tape, attach cups to sides of helmet and thermometer on top. Use small squares of black tape to create pattern around helmet.

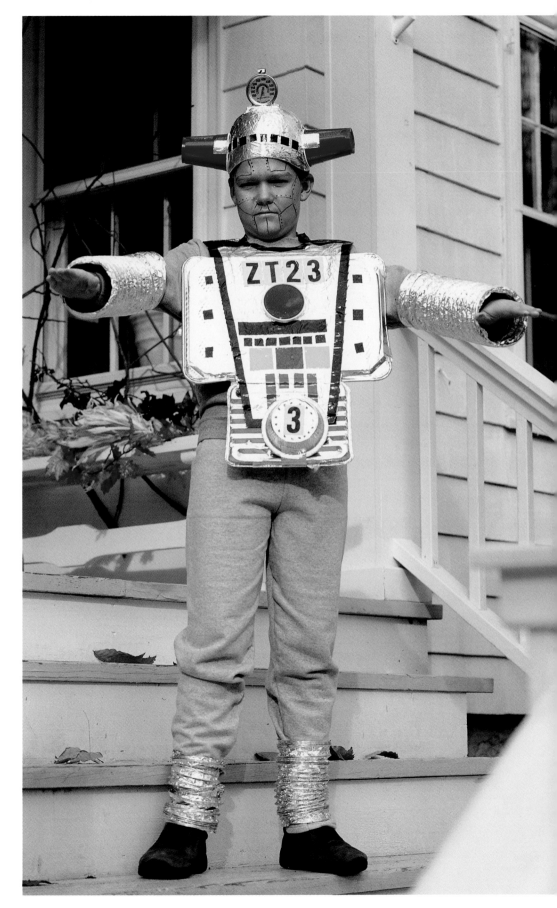

Wizard

SKILL LEVEL: Intermediate

MATERIALS: 2 yards of turquoise satin fabric; scissors; hot-glue gun and fabric glue sticks; 13 inches of Velcro brand Fabric Fusion tape; iron; press cloth; flat-back faux gemstones; 1 yard of silver metallic fabric; remnants of purple satin; 1 yard of purple tulle fabric; 8 inches square of white card stock; pencil; 14-inch piece of ⅜-inch dowel; metallic silver spray paint; five 1-yard lengths of assorted ribbons and trims; 4 yards of coordinating blue damask satin fabric.

DIRECTIONS:

1 Enlarge dress pattern, opposite, top (see *How to Enlarge Patterns*, page 128). Cut twice from turquoise satin fabric for front and back.

2 With right sides facing and raw edges even, glue front to back at sides and shoulder edges to make dress.

3 Turn under 1 inch on neck, wrist and lower edges and glue to hem dress.

4 Cut 10-inch slit at center back neck of dress. Cut 10-inch piece of Velcro. Separate tape sections. Place one piece fusible side up on ironing board; place one cut edge of dress over tape. Cover with press cloth; using iron on high steam setting, press for 1 minute to bond tape to dress. Fuse other piece of tape to other cut edge of dress in same manner so ends can fasten when overlapped.

5 Glue gems to wrists and neck edge.

6 Enlarge hat pattern, opposite, bottom (see *How to Enlarge Patterns*, page 128). Cut twice from metallic fabric for hat and lining.

7 With right sides facing and raw edges even, glue lining to hat, leaving small opening along one long edge for turning. Turn right side out. Roll into cone shape, overlapping back edges; glue closed to make hat.

8 Cut star and moon shapes from purple satin remnants; glue onto hat.

9 Gather up one short end of tulle; glue to point of hat. Glue gems to cover end of tulle.

10 To make wand, draw large star on card stock; cut out. Glue star to end of dowel. Spray-paint wand silver; let dry.

11 Glue gems to front of star. Glue ribbons to back of star for streamers.

12 To make cape, cut damask in half crosswise. Overlap and glue selvages together to make one wide piece. Fold in quarters. Starting at folded corner, measure 34 inches and mark curved line along fabric; cut out to make 68-inch circle. Measure and mark 5-inch curved line at point in same manner; cut out to make 10-inch circle for neck opening.

13 Slit cape from center to edge. Turn under 1 inch on all raw edges and glue to hem cape.

14 Cut 3-inch piece of Velcro. Separate tape sections. Place one piece fusible side up on ironing board; place one neck edge of cape over tape. Cover with press cloth; using iron on high steam setting, press for 1 minute to bond tape to cape. Fuse other piece of tape to other cut edge of cape in same manner so ends can fasten when overlapped.

15 Put dress, hat and cape on child.

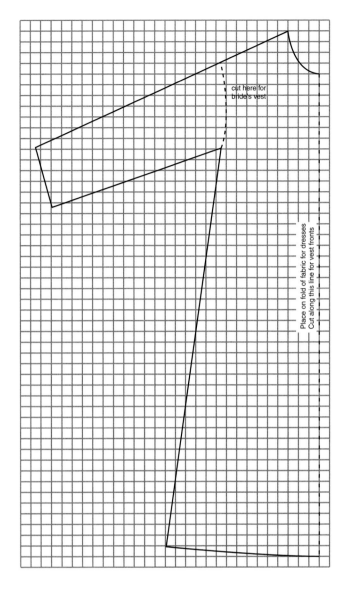

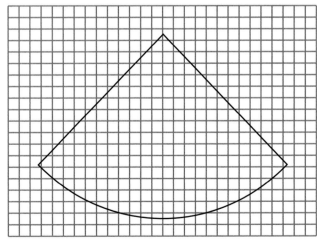

one square = 1 inch

DIRECTIONS:

1 Enlarge vest front and back patterns, below (see *How to Enlarge Patterns*, page 128). From purple satin, cut 2 fronts (for front and lining) and 2 backs.

2 With right sides facing and raw edges even, glue 2 backs to front at sides and shoulder edges. Turn under ½ inch on all edges and glue to hem vest. To line front, turn under ½ inch on all edges of lining and glue, wrong sides facing, to front.

3 Cut Velcro tape to back length of vest. Separate sections. Glue one piece, right side down, along one back center edge of vest. Glue other piece, right side up, along other back edge of vest so edges can fasten when overlapped.

4 Glue buttons to front of vest.

5 With right sides facing and raw edges even, stitch red and black satin together along long edges, using ½-inch seam. Stitch upper 5 inches of each short end, leave open 1½ inches, then stitch to lower edge. Turn right side out to make cape.

6 Starting 5 inches from upper edge, sew across cape through both layers. Starting 1½ inches below stitching line, make another stitching line in same manner to form casing (aligns with unstitched area on each side of cape).

7 Attach safety pin to one end of black ribbon; pull through casing. Gather up cape so ribbon extends 5 inches on each end of cape. Cut 5 inches of Velcro tape. Separate sections. Glue pieces to ribbon ends so ends can fasten when overlapped. To make medallion, cut card stock in star shape. Glue gems to medallion. Glue center of red ribbon to back of medallion.

8 Dress child in white shirt, sweatpants, vest and cape. Tie medallion around neck.

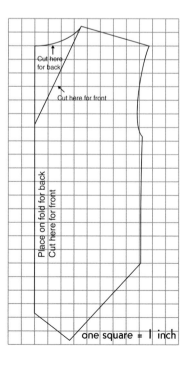

Cut here for back

Cut here for front

Place on fold for back
Cut here for front

one square = 1 inch

Delightful Dracula

SKILL LEVEL: Intermediate

MATERIALS: 1 yard of purple satin fabric; 2 yards of red satin fabric; 2 yards of black satin fabric; scissors; hot-glue gun and fabric glue sticks; ½ yard of Velcro brand black Sew-On tape, 1 inch wide; five ½-inch black or gold buttons; hand-sewing needle and black thread; 1 yard of black ribbon, 1 inch wide; safety pin; remnant of white card stock; 1 yard of red satin ribbon, 2 inches wide; red flat-back gemstones; white shirt with collar; black sweatpants.

Dapper Skeleton

SKILL LEVEL: Intermediate

MATERIALS: Black sweatshirt and sweatpants; scissors; ¼ yard of Velcro brand Fabric Fusion tape; iron; press cloth; 4 yards of Velcro brand white Sew-On tape, 1 ½ inches wide; hot-glue gun and fabric glue sticks; 9 x 12-inch piece of red felt; small felt or fabric remnants in assorted colors; 1 yard of green sequin fabric; pinking shears; ⅛ yard of purple tulle or chiffon fabric; waxed paper; foam paintbrush; liquid fabric stiffener; hand-sewing needle and thread; purple glitter spray; purchased black suit jacket (thrift store), gloves, cane and sequined top hat.

DIRECTIONS:

1 Cut 8-inch slit at center back neck of sweatshirt. Cut 8-inch piece of Velcro fusion tape. Separate tape sections. Place one piece fusible side up on ironing board; place one cut edge of shirt over tape. Cover with press cloth; using iron on high steam setting, press for 1 minute to bond tape to shirt. Fuse other piece of tape to other cut edge of shirt in same manner so ends can fasten when overlapped.

2 Cut bone shapes from Velcro sew-on tape; glue to front of sweatshirt, along sleeves and down pant legs to resemble skeleton. Enlarge necktie pattern, right (see *How to Enlarge Patterns*, page 128); cut necktie from red felt. Cut polka dots from felt remnants; glue dots to tie. Use remaining 1-inch piece of Velcro fusion tape to attach tie to neck bone on sweatshirt.

3 Cut a piece of sequin fabric, using jacket neck and lapels as pattern. Glue fabric over neck and lapels.

4 To make flower, use pinking shears to cut 8 circles from purple fabric, making largest about 4 inches across and smallest about 1 inch across. Place circles on waxed paper; brush with fabric stiffener. Let dry, then turn over and brush other side in same manner. Let dry. Layer circles in graduated order, with smallest on top, and stitch through center to secure.

5 Scrunch circles to make flower shape; spray with glitter. Let dry. Glue flower to lapel.

6 Dress child in costume, then accessorize with gloves, cane and hat.

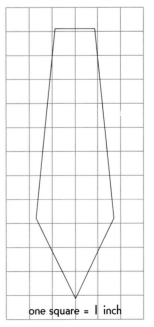

one square = 1 inch

LITTLE WORKSHOP OF HORRORS: CREEPY CRAFTS

Halloween projects that you create yourself immediately put family and friends in the mood as they enter your home. These attention-grabbing designs are easy to make and can be reused for years of haunting celebrations.

Visitors will never know that the chilled Jars of Yuck (for instructions, turn to page 74) they're sticking their hands in started as common household items: jarred pearl onions, cooked pasta, and mushy cauliflower. "Ghostly smoke" from dry ice, fake bones and a scary rubber hand complete the tableau.

Jars of Yuck

SKILL LEVEL: Beginner

MATERIALS: Curly spaghetti, cooked; liquid food coloring: red, yellow; head of cauliflower; serrated knife; jar of pearl onions; rubber hand; plastic skulls and bones; glass jars and beakers; self-adhesive labels; fine-point permanent black marker; cake stands; fake spider webs.

DIRECTIONS:

1 **To make intestines:** Mix spaghetti with red food coloring; place in jar and cover jar tightly.

2 **To make brains:** Trim stem off cauliflower; trim cauliflower into brain shape. Place in jar; add water and small amount of yellow food coloring. Cover jar tightly; shake to disburse color.

3 **To make eyeballs:** Remove label from jar of pearl onions.

4 Place rubber hand in a jar; fill with water. Cover jar tightly.

5 Place skulls and bones in jar; fill with water. Cover jar tightly.

6 Write contents on labels; adhere to jars. Arrange jars on cake stands. Drape spider webs over arrangement.

FAR RIGHT: Fill glass containers of all shapes and sizes with a selection of rubber rats, plastic insects, almonds, fake bones and skulls. For labels, follow instructions for the invitations, below.

NEAR RIGHT: Write invitations on a computer with a Gothic font and print out. Tear edges into the shape you want, crumple into a ball and drop into a cup of coffee. Squeeze out and let dry. Cut out bone shapes from craft paper or a paper bag and paste on. Buy brown envelopes for mailing.

Mini Candy Corn Buckets

SKILL LEVEL: Beginner

MATERIALS: Small peat moss cup (available at garden-supply stores); assorted paintbrushes; acrylic paints: white, orange, yellow; scissors; pipe cleaners: yellow, orange; craft glue or hot-glue gun.

DIRECTIONS:

1 Paint cup inside and out with several coats of white paint, letting dry after each coat.

2 Using smaller flat brush, paint a yellow stripe around top of each cup and an orange stripe around middle of each cup to resemble candy corn; let dry.

3 Cut a pipe cleaner of each color in half. Twist 2 different-color pieces together to form striped handle. Bend ends of handles to form small loops.

4 Glue handle loops inside upper edges of cups. Fill cup as desired.

Party Buckets

SKILL LEVEL: Beginner

MATERIALS: Sharp pencil; cardboard paint bucket; felt: orange, black; scissors; tacky craft glue; small glass bowl; foam paintbrush; assorted trims such as ball fringe and pom-poms; black paper twist ribbon.

DIRECTIONS:

1 Using pencil, poke holes in opposite sides of bucket, about 1 inch from top, for handles.

2 Cut desired felt to fit sides of bucket. Cut desired decorative shapes from contrasting felt.

3 In glass bowl, mix glue with small amount of water to thin it slightly. Brush a coat of thinned glue onto sides of bucket; cover with felt, smoothing from center out to eliminate air bubbles. Glue felt pieces, fringe and pom-poms to bucket as desired.

4 When all trim is dry, use tip of scissors to poke holes through felt covering bucket holes. Slip one end of paper twist ribbon through one hole; knot end. Slip other end of paper through other hole to make handle of desired length. Knot other end of paper. Fill bucket as desired.

These lovely Mini Candy Corn Buckets make a sweet addition to all your decorating projects. They also do double duty as party favors filled to the brim with the holiday's traditional candy they resemble.

Candy Corn Garland

SKILL LEVEL: Beginner

MATERIALS: Sculpey III oven-bake polymer clay: Just Orange, yellow, white, Granny Smith; ruler; nonstick work mat; ½-inch Lucite dowel or nonstick rolling pin; craft knife; cutting mat; large embroidery needle; cookie sheet; oven; baking rack; skein of black embroidery floss.

DIRECTIONS:

1 Roll 1¼-inch ball of Just Orange, 1-inch ball of yellow and 1-inch ball of white; roll each ball into 6-inch-long log. With rolling pin, flatten each log to ¼-inch thick strips.

2 Place strips on work surface; align and press yellow strip to top of Just Orange strip and white strip to bottom of Just Orange strip. Smooth edges where strips meet.

3 Place clay on cutting mat. Cut triangles from clay, making yellow bottom end about ¾ inch wide and coming to point at white top end. Make 8 pieces of candy corn in this manner.

4 Roll nine 9/16-inch balls of Granny Smith for spacer beads.

5 To make holes in candy corn and beads, insert needle through candy corn just below yellow section or through center of bead. When point of needle begins to emerge, remove needle and push through from other side. Rotate clay on needle to enlarge hole slightly; remove needle.

6 Place pieces on baking rack; bake according to clay manufacturer's directions.

7 Place on rack to cool.

8 Thread pieces onto floss, starting and ending with bead. Space pieces about 2 inches apart and tie large knot in floss before and after each piece to hold in place.

Invite youngsters to trim a black Halloween tree from a craft store with creepy ornaments and a Candy Corn Garland they make themselves.

Ghost Wall Hanging

SKILL LEVEL: Beginner

MATERIALS: Tracing paper; pencil; scissors; 2½ yards of Heat n' Bond paper-backed fusible web; felt: ¾ yard black, ½ yard green, ½ yard white, ½ yard orange, remnants of purple and yellow; ruler; chalk fabric marking pencil; iron; 2½-inch piece of white Velcro Fabric Fusion tape; Beacon Fabri-Tac fabric glue; 20 inches of Velcro Décor tape.

DIRECTIONS:

1 Enlarge Ghost Wall Hanging pattern, below (see *How to Enlarge Patterns*, page 128). Trace each section of pattern onto tracing paper and cut out to make templates.

2 Trace each template onto paper side of Heat n'Bond, leaving 1 inch between pieces. Cut out each piece, leaving ½-inch margin of paper on each.

3 Measure, mark and cut 20 x 25-inch piece of black felt for backing.

4 With iron, fuse web onto felt as follows: ghost onto white, window bars onto green, curtains onto orange, stars onto yellow, and eyes, nose and mouth onto black. Cut out each piece along outlines. Also cut about thirty ¼ x 2-inch strips of purple felt for curtain decorations.

5 Cut another piece of white felt to correspond with ghost's finger as marked on pattern.

6 Peel off paper backing of all pieces. Fuse additional cutout finger behind ghost's finger. Arrange pieces on backing, starting with ghost and layering window bars, curtains, stars and facial features on top. Fuse in place. Finger will not adhere to backing.

7 Separate sections of Velcro Fabric Fusion tape; fuse loop section to back of ghost's finger and hook section to backing behind finger.

8 Turn under 2 inches on upper edges of backing; glue in place to hem.

9 Press Velcro Décor tape onto back of hem. Peel off paper backing and press tape onto display surface. Wall hanging is easily removed for storage.

This spooky felt Ghost Wall Hanging looks great displayed like a painting, and even better peeking out from behind a glass door or window. You could even use it to cover a mirror.

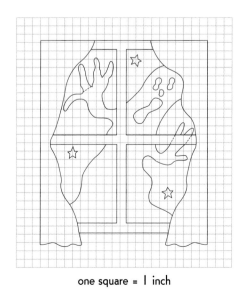

one square = 1 inch

3-D Bats and Pumpkins Hanging

SKILL LEVEL: Beginner

MATERIALS: Tracing paper; pencil; scissors; 1 yard of Heat n' Bond paper-backed fusible web; felt: ¾ yard purple, ½ yard black, ½ yard green, ¼ yard white, ¼ yard orange, ½ yard yellow; ruler; chalk fabric marking pencil; iron; hole punch; Beacon Fabri-Tac fabric glue; 6-inch piece of black Velcro Fabric Fusion tape; 19 inches of Velcro Décor tape.

DIRECTIONS:

1 Enlarge 3-D Bats and Pumpkins Hanging pattern, right (see *How to Enlarge Patterns*, page 128). Trace each section of pattern (including checkerboard but not bats) onto tracing paper and cut out to make templates.

one square = 1 inch

2 Trace each template onto paper side of Heat n'Bond, leaving 1 inch between pieces. Cut out each piece, leaving ½ inch margin of paper on each.

3 Measure, mark and cut 19 x 27-inch piece of purple felt for backing.

4 With iron, fuse web onto felt as follows: pumpkin noses, mouths and eye centers onto black; half of checkerboard squares, small pumpkin, medium pumpkin teeth and large pumpkin eyes onto green; small pumpkin eyes and medium pumpkin onto white; medium pumpkin eyes and large pumpkin onto orange; stars, pumpkin stem, half of checkerboard squares and large pumpkin teeth onto yellow. Cut out each piece along outlines. Cut three black bats, six ½-inch yellow circles for bat eyes and three 2 x 12-inch black strips for bat supports.

5 Peel off paper backing of all pieces. Arrange pieces on backing, starting with checkerboard pattern at lower edge and layering pumpkins, stars and facial features on top. Fuse in place.

6 Punch 2 holes on each bat for eyes. Glue yellow circles under holes.

You don't have to know how to sew to make our 3-D Bats and Pumpkins Hanging. All you need is colored felt and Velcro Brand Fabric Fusion. It takes a little time to cut out the patterns and put them together, but you'll have this enchanting decoration for years to come.

7 Roll bat support strips like jelly rolls; glue to secure. Glue support to center back of bat.

8 Cut 3 equal pieces of Velcro Fabric Fusion tape; separate sections. Fuse loop sections to ends of supports and hook sections to backing at each X mark. Press bats onto X marks for three-dimensional effect.

9 Turn under 2 inches on upper edges of backing; glue in place to hem.

10 Press Velcro Décor tape onto back of hem. Peel off paper backing and press tape onto display surface. Wall hanging is easily removed for storage.

Phantom Frames

Snap individual digital pictures of the children in their costumes. Print out and give each child his photo and a foam-board frame you've preassembled to decorate. Make it easy by having plenty of colorful markers and store-bought stickers on hand. When the creations are complete, affix magnetic tape to the backs. Presto! Instant portraits to take home for the fridge as party favors.

Glowing Ghost

SKILL LEVEL: Beginner

MATERIALS: Premo Sculpey oven-bake polymer clay: Glow-in-the-Dark; ruler; nonstick work mat; ½-inch Lucite dowel or nonstick rolling pin; toothpicks; cookie sheet; oven; baking rack; craft glue; pumpkin; black spray paint.

DIRECTIONS:

1 Roll ⅞-inch ball of clay with a dowel or rolling pin on a nonstick work mat; shape ends to form slightly pointed oval for body.

2 Round out top point to form head. Press in sides of clay to form neck. Pull up on sides to form arms. Roll bottom point to make it narrower and shape into a curve.

3 Using toothpick, poke 2 holes near top of head for eyes. Poke larger hole for mouth.

4 Poke hole in bottom of ghost; remove toothpick.

5 Place ghost on baking rack; bake according to clay manufacturer's directions.

6 Place on rack to cool.

7 Glue toothpick into bottom hole.

8 Apply several thin, even coats of paint to pumpkin, letting dry after each coat.

9 Poke toothpicks into pumpkin.

Clay Creations Every partygoer gets to use his imagination to the fullest when it comes to creating spooktacular clay decorations.

An adorable Glowing Ghost rides high atop a sturdy fake flower stem or green toothpick. Poked in a pumpkin, he appears to be hovering in mid-flight. He's made of special glow-in-the-dark clay so he can fly at night, too. But why stop at just one? He's so cute, make a whole bunch.

Black Cat

SKILL LEVEL: Beginner

MATERIALS: Sculpey III oven-bake polymer clay: black, Granny Smith, white; ruler; nonstick work mat; ½-inch Lucite dowel or nonstick rolling pin; toothpick; 1-inch length of thin black wire; cookie sheet; oven; baking rack.

DIRECTIONS:

1 Using a dowel or rolling pin, roll ⅞-inch ball of black on nonstick work mat; form into 2½-inch-long log for body. Fold in half and pinch ends together, keeping upper portion rounded for cat's back.

2 Roll ⅝-inch ball of black; press onto front of body to form head.

3 Roll ½-inch ball of black; roll into tapered log. Press smaller end of log onto back of body to form tail.

4 Roll two ¼-inch balls of black; press onto tapered bottom of body to form feet.

5 Roll two ¼-inch balls of black; shape into rounded triangles and press onto sides of head to form ears. Indent centers slightly to shape ears.

6 Roll two ⅛-inch balls of black; press onto face to make muzzle.

7 Roll ⅛-inch ball of Granny Smith; press just above muzzle for nose.

8 Roll two ⅛-inch balls of white; form into fangs and press onto muzzle so they point down.

9 Roll several tiny balls of black; press onto top of head to form hair.

10 Using toothpick, draw texture on tail and form toes on feet.

11 To make hanging loop, bend wire in half; twist ends together. Push ends into top of back so loop extends at top.

12 Place ornament on baking rack; bake according to clay manufacturer's directions.

13 Place on rack to cool.

This adorable Black Cat is crafted of black clay. With a sweet green clay nose and white fangs to boot, this much friendlier version of a Halloween cat will have your trick-or-treaters wishing he was real.

This Grouchy Ghost looks like he doesn't want the night to end. After sculpting his expressive face and shape, insert a wire hanger so he can "fly" from a branch.

Witch's Hat

SKILL LEVEL: Beginner

MATERIALS: Sculpey III oven-bake polymer clay: black, Just Orange, Granny Smith; ruler; nonstick work mat; ½-inch Lucite dowel or nonstick rolling pin; toothpick; 1-inch length of thin black wire; cookie sheet; oven; baking rack.

DIRECTIONS:

1 Using a dowel or rolling pin, roll ¾-inch ball of black on a nonstick work mat; form into triangle shape about ¼-inch thick to form hat.

2 Roll ¾-inch ball of black; flatten into circle and fold in half to form brim.

3 Press wide end of hat onto straight edge of brim.

4 Roll ¼-inch ball of Just Orange; roll into thin rope. Press to base of hat to form hatband. Trim off excess band at ends of hat.

5 Roll ¼-inch ball of Granny Smith; form into crescent moon shape and press onto hat brim.

6 To make hanging loop, bend wire in half; twist ends together. Push ends into top of hat so loop extends at top.

7 Place ornament on baking rack; bake according to clay manufacturer's directions.

8 Place on rack to cool.

Grouchy Ghost

SKILL LEVEL: Beginner

MATERIALS: Sculpey III oven-bake polymer clay: white, Granny Smith; ruler; nonstick work mat; ½-inch Lucite dowel or nonstick rolling pin; toothpick; 1-inch length of thin black wire; cookie sheet; oven; baking rack.

DIRECTIONS:

1 Using a dowel or rolling pin, roll 1-inch ball of white on a nonstick work mat; shape ends to form slightly pointed oval for body.

2 Round out top point to form head. Pull up on sides to form arms. Roll bottom point to make it narrower and shape into a curve.

3 Poke 2 holes near top of head for eyes. Poke larger hole for mouth; using toothpick, pull down and shape lower edge to form bottom lip.

4 Roll two ⅛-inch balls of Granny Smith; form into small logs and press above eyes to form eyebrows.

5 To make hanging loop, bend wire in half; twist ends together. Push ends into top of head so loop extends at top.

6 Place ornament on baking rack; bake according to clay manufacturer's directions.

7 Place on rack to cool.

This quirky Witch's Hat with its colorful decorations makes a fashion statement. To make, bend black clay into hat shape, then adorn with orange and green clay accents.

Frankenstein

SKILL LEVEL: Beginner

MATERIALS: Sculpey III oven-bake polymer clay: Granny Smith, black, silver; ruler; nonstick work mat; ½-inch Lucite dowel or nonstick rolling pin; toothpick; 1-inch length of thin black wire; cookie sheet; oven; baking rack.

DIRECTIONS:

1 Using a dowel or rolling pin, roll ⅞-inch ball of Granny Smith on a nonstick work mat; press into teardrop shape, then press narrow end flat to form lightbulb shape for head.

2 Roll ¼-inch ball of Granny Smith; roll into ½-inch-long log. Press onto center of forehead for brows; smooth ends to blend into face.

3 Roll ¼-inch ball of Granny Smith; press just below brow for nose.

4 Roll two ⅛-inch balls of Granny Smith; press to sides of head for ears. Press indentation into center of each ear.

5 Roll ½-inch ball of black; press into cube. Press onto top of head to make hair.

6 Roll two ⅛-inch balls of silver; roll into small pointed logs. Press into sides of head to make bolts.

7 Using toothpick, draw smile and scars on face. Draw texture lines on hair.

8 To make hanging loop, bend wire in half; twist ends together. Push ends into top of head so loop extends at top.

9 Place ornament on baking rack; bake according to clay manufacturer's directions.

10 Place on rack to cool.

With a green clay face and black clay hair, and finished with orange clay bolts and toothpick-drawn scars and hairdo, Frankenstein is ready to party.

Who ever heard of Halloween without a mummy? This Grave Guy is made in two steps. First, shape the head and face out of green clay. Then, roll out and cut white clay into strips for "bandages." Wrap strips around the face and insert beady black clay eyes to peer out.

Grave Guy

SKILL LEVEL: Beginner

MATERIALS: Sculpey III oven-bake polymer clay: Granny Smith, black, white; ruler; nonstick work mat; ½-inch Lucite dowel or nonstick rolling pin; toothpick; craft knife; cutting mat; 1-inch length of thin black wire; cookie sheet; oven; baking rack.

DIRECTIONS:

1 Using a dowel or rolling pin, roll ⅞-inch ball of Granny Smith on a nonstick work mat; flatten back by pressing against work mat to make head.

2 Roll ¼-inch ball of Granny Smith; press onto center of head for nose. Using toothpick, poke 2 holes above nose for eyes.

3 Roll two ⅛-inch balls of black; press above eyes to form eyebrows.

4 Roll out white to about ⅛-inch thick; place on cutting mat and use craft knife to cut assorted 15¼-inch strips. Press strips across face, leaving eyes and part of nose exposed. Trim off excess at sides of head.

5 To make hanging loop, bend wire in half; twist ends together. Push ends into top of head so loop extends at top.

6 Place ornament on baking rack; bake according to clay manufacturer's directions.

7 Place on rack to cool.

A little bit of felt, some fabric glue and Velcro Brand Fabric Fusion is all it takes to make these Spooky Tiebacks, which you can use on regular draperies or on the custom window treatments shown on page 29.

Spooky Tiebacks

SKILL LEVEL: Beginner

MATERIALS: (for two tiebacks): Tracing paper; pencil; scissors; felt: ½ yard white, remnants of black and green; chalk fabric marking pencil; Beacon Fabri-tac fabric glue; 6-inch piece of white Velcro Fabric Fusion tape; iron.

DIRECTIONS:

1 Enlarge Spooky Tieback pattern, below, onto tracing paper (see *How to Enlarge Patterns*, page 128); cut out pattern.

2 Using pattern, cut 2 ghosts from white felt, 2 outer eyes from black felt, 2 inner eyes from green felt, 1 nose from black felt and 1 mouth from black felt. Mark positions of facial features on ghost with chalk pencil.

3 Glue facial features onto ghost.

4 Cut Fabric Fusion into 2 equal pieces; separate sections.

5 With iron, fuse a hook section onto one extension on each ghost, centered on wrong side of felt.

6 Fuse loop sections onto other extensions on each ghost, centered on right side of felt.

7 Wrap tieback around curtain; press Velcro strips together to secure.

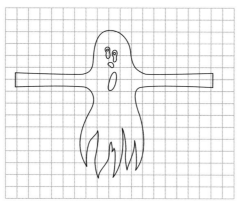

one square = 1 inch

Eyeball Fern

SKILL LEVEL: Beginner

MATERIALS: Small white glass marbles; fine paintbrush; glass paint; fronds of artificial ferns; scissors; hot-glue gun and glue sticks; artificial fern plant in pot.

DIRECTIONS:

1 On each marble, paint eye details to make eyes; let dry.

2 Cut eyelid shapes from fern fronds; glue an eyelid onto each eye.

3 Glue eyeballs onto plant's stems or leaves.

White glass marbles and a little glass paint from a craft store are turned into an eyeful of frightening "flowers" on this Eyeball Fern. Faux ferns create the glued-on eyelids; once the eyes are assembled, attach them to a prepared silk plant base with a green wire stem.

These purr-fect felines put a friendly scare into the festivities and are great for a children's party activity. Black Cats on a Stick have raffia whiskers, button eyes and felt ears, nose and mouth.

Black Cats on a Stick

SKILL LEVEL: Beginner

MATERIALS: Black paper plates; sharp scissors; felt: black, yellow, orange; hot-glue gun and glue sticks; 2 white buttons; raffia; long craft or popsicle stick.

DIRECTIONS:

1 Cut outer edges of plate in jagged pattern.

2 From felt, cut 2 black triangle ears, 1 small yellow triangle nose and 1 orange oval mouth.

3 Glue ears to back upper edge of plate. Glue nose to center front of plate. Glue mouth below nose.

4 Using tip of scissors, poke a hole in plate on each side of nose.

5 Thread several strands of raffia through holes to form whiskers; trim to desired length. Glue to back of plate.

6 Glue buttons to plate for eyes.

7 Glue stick to back of plate so stick extends below plate.

Treat Cups

SKILL LEVEL: Beginner

MATERIALS: Large candy or ice cream cups; sheets of crepe paper: orange, black; scissors; craft glue; pipe cleaners: black, white, orange; candy.

DIRECTIONS:

1 Place cup in center of crepe paper. Cut paper in circle large enough that paper edges extend 4 inches above top of cup.

2 Apply a dot of glue to center of paper; press bottom of cup into glue. Let dry.

3 Fill cup with candy; twist paper above candy to secure. Wrap pipe cleaner around paper to hold it shut. Coil ends of pipe cleaner as desired.

4 Cut top of paper into fringe; fan out fringe. Cut strip of contrasting crepe paper to fit around cup. Wrap and glue paper around cup.

These terrific Treat Cups are easily made with small cardboard ice cream scoop cups, orange and black crepe paper and white pipe cleaners to safely seal off the sweets inside.

Halloween Bingo This version is like regular bingo only wackier. Print game cards filled with holiday icons on bright orange paper. To create theme-related game pieces, buy inexpensive spider rings and cut off the ring part. Or, substitute candy corn (toss it away after the party). Put on spooky music to enhance the Halloween atmosphere while you do the calling. When a child completes a row, he hollers out something like "Yikes!" as in "I've just seen a ghost!" Have a basket of prizes wrapped in orange tissue ready for winners.

Your Haunted House Apron will scare off anyone who dares to think of playing a trick on you this All Hallows Eve. Trick-or-treaters will delight in its wickedly fun design. Come to the door holding a large pot with a Wanna Bite? Cauldron Cover to complete the effect.

Haunted House Apron

SKILL LEVEL: Beginner

MATERIALS: Tracing paper; pencil; scissors; felt: ½ yard black, remnants of white, purple, yellow; ½ yard Heat n' Bond paper-backed fusible web; iron; 30-inch piece of Velcro brand Fabric Fusion no-sew tape; orange cotton apron; Fabri-tac by Beacon fabric glue; 4 small black flat-back beads.

NOTE: Remove appliqué before washing apron.

DIRECTIONS:

1 Enlarge haunted house pattern, below (see *How to Enlarge Patterns*, page 128). Trace ghosts, ghost mouths, windows and door onto Heat n' Bond; cut out, leaving ½-inch margin around each piece. From black felt, cut entire house, including ghosts, for base.

2 With iron, fuse ghosts onto white felt, ghost mouths onto black felt, door onto purple felt and window sections onto yellow felt; cut out. Peel off paper backing and arrange ghosts, door and windows on base. Fuse in place.

3 Cut Velcro into three equal pieces; separate sections. Fuse loop sections to back of base, near sides and down center. Place base as desired on center front of apron; mark Velcro placement. Fuse hook sections to apron where marked.

4 Glue beads to ghosts for eyes.

Wanna Bite? Cauldron Cover

SKILL LEVEL: Beginner

MATERIALS: Medium metal pot for base; tape measure; chalk marking pencil; scissors; felt: ½ yard green, ⅜ yard purple, remnants of orange and black; Fabri-tac by Beacon fabric glue; 12-inch piece of Velcro brand Fabric Fusion no-sew tape; pins; iron; ½ yard of Heat n' Bond paper-backed fusible web.

DIRECTIONS:

1 Measure canister height; add 1 inch. Measure around canister; add 1½ inches. Mark and cut green felt to these measurements for cover.

2 Turn under ½ inch on upper and lower edges; glue.

3 Separate Velcro sections. With iron, fuse one section to right side of cover, centering it along one raw edge. Pin other section to wrong side of cover, centering it along other raw edge. Wrap cover around pot to check fit; adjust pins as needed and mark placement. Remove pins and fuse in place.

4 Enlarge witch hands and lettering pattern, below (see *How to Enlarge Patterns*, page 128). Trace each pattern onto Heat n' Bond; cut out, leaving ½-inch margin around each piece. Fuse letters onto black felt, hands onto purple felt and fingernails onto orange felt; cut out. Peel off paper backing and arrange letters, hands and nails on center front of cover. Fuse in place.

5 Wrap and secure cover around canister.

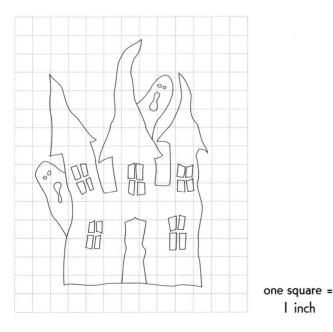

one square =
1 inch

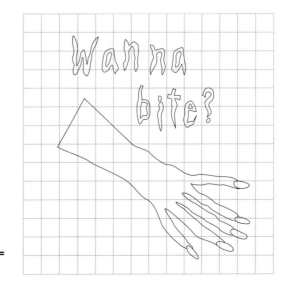

Pin the Spider on the Web

SKILL LEVEL: Beginner

MATERIALS: 30-inch square of ¼-inch foamcore board; 1 yard of orange cotton fabric; masking tape; package of polyester spiderweb; hot-glue gun; scissors; old magazine; black acrylic spray paint; silk vines; plastic cups: black, orange; awl or sharp scissors; black pipe cleaners; medium google eyes; red medium-point permanent marker; self-adhesive picture hook; 12 inches of black yarn.

DIRECTIONS:

1 Place board in center of fabric; wrap and tape fabric edges to wrong side of board, folding in fullness at corners.

2 Stretch web over right side of board; glue edges to back of board.

3 Cut letters out of old magazine to spell "BOO" and glue to front of board as desired.

4 Paint vines; let dry.

5 To make spiders, use awl or scissors to poke 4 holes on each side of each cup, near lower edge. Push a pipe cleaner through each pair of cup holes to form legs (8 legs total). Bend lower legs into hook shapes for feet; hooks will adhere to polyester web when children play game.

6 Glue google eyes on each spider; write child's initials in red on cup to identify piece when playing.

7 Attach hook to wall where game will be played. Knot ends of yarn together; glue knotted end to back of board to form hanging loop. Hang game on wall. Hot-glue vines to wall around edges of board.

Treat Yourself Let tricksters design their very own party favors. Buy orange containers and a variety of materials such as sticky-back letters and plastic spider webs at a craft store. Position bowls of candy around the room, and have young guests fill up the containers right before they leave for home.

Pin the Spider on the Web is an easy-to-make, fanciful variation on the traditional donkey game. All you'll need is orange fabric, foam-core board, fake fuzzy spiders, orange and black cups, black pipe cleaners and a plastic chenille spider web from a craft store. Be sure to put children's initials on the bottom of cups to identify spider game players.

Bread "Branch" Sticks

MAKES: 8
PREP: 10 min
BAKE: 12–15 min

    3 Tbsp sesame seeds
    2 Tbsp poppy seeds
    2 tsp Kosher salt
    ¼ tsp cayenne pepper (optional)
    2 tubes (8 oz each) plain refrigerated bread sticks

1 Preheat oven to 375°F. Coat two baking sheets with nonstick cooking spray; set aside. Combine the sesame seeds, poppy seeds, salt and cayenne pepper in a small bowl.

2 Sprinkle 1 Tbsp of the seed mixture onto a clean work surface. Unwrap one tube of bread-stick dough and arrange bread sticks on top of seeds. Make a 3-in. cut, lengthwise, into each strip of dough. Sprinkle tops of bread sticks with a generous tablespoon of seed mixture. Twist pieces and separate cut to look like branches. Arrange dough pieces on prepared sheet pans. Repeat with remaining dough and seeds.

3 Bake until golden; about 12 to 15 minutes. Transfer to a wire rack and cool completely.

Spicy Cornbread Sticks

MAKES: 14 (or 10 muffins)
PREP: 10 min
BAKE: 10–12 min (sticks); 15–20 min (muffins)

    1¼ cups flour
    ¾ cup yellow cornmeal
    2 Tbsp sugar
    2 tsp baking powder
    ½ tsp salt
    ⅛ tsp cayenne pepper
    1 cup milk
    ⅓ cup vegetable oil
    1 large egg

1 Preheat oven to 400°F. Coat two corn stick pans or 10 cups in a muffin pan with nonstick spray.

2 Combine flour, cornmeal, sugar, baking powder, salt and cayenne pepper in a medium bowl. In another bowl, whisk milk, oil and egg. Pour milk mixture over the flour mixture. Stir just until combined.

3 Spoon batter into pans until each mold is two-thirds full. Bake 10 to 12 minutes (sticks) and 15 to 20 minutes (muffins) until golden brown. Transfer to wire rack; cool 3 minutes. Invert onto rack.

Sand-Witches

MAKES: 12
PREP: 20 min
COOK: 3 min per batch

12 slices white bread
12 slices pumpernickel bread
24 slices cheese, such as cheddar, provolone
   or Swiss
12 slices baked ham or turkey
6 Tbsp butter, softened
2 Tbsp vegetable oil
1 roasted red pepper, cut into thin strips
Yellow mustard
Parsley for garnish

1 Cover two baking sheets with nonstick foil or parchment paper; set aside.

2 Cut bread slices, cheese and ham or turkey with a witch-hat cookie cutter, or other desired shape. Spread the softened butter over one side of each slice of bread.

3 Place a piece of buttered bread on prepared baking sheet, buttered side down. Top with 2 slices of cheese and 1 slice of meat. Top with some of the cheese scraps followed by another piece of buttered bread, buttered side up. Repeat layering with the remaining bread, cheese and meat.

4 Preheat oven to 250°F. Heat 2 tsp oil in a large nonstick skillet over medium heat. Add as many sandwiches as will fit. Cook until bottom of bread is lightly toasted; about 1 to 2 minutes. Turn sandwiches over and cook until golden, about 1 minute longer. Transfer to baking sheet. Place in the oven while cooking the other sandwiches to keep warm. Continue with the remaining sandwiches.

5 Decorate sandwiches with a slice of red pepper or a line of mustard along the brim just before serving. Garnish platter with parsley.

Grilled cheese Sand-Witches filled with ham or turkey on pumpernickel and white bread are the tops when you stamp them out with a cookie cutter, then toast them up in a skillet. Yellow mustard and roasted red pepper add all the color and flavor you need.

Crude-ités with Green Slime Dip

SERVES: 12
PREP: 25 min
COOK: 1 min

DIP
1 cup packed basil leaves
¼ cup packed parsley leaves
1 clove garlic
2 scallions, chopped
½ cup *each* sour cream and mayonnaise
Salt and freshly ground black pepper to taste
Green food coloring (optional)

CRUDE-ITÉS
1 bunch celery
1 head Belgian endive, separated into leaves
1 head radicchio
1 lb carrots, cut into sticks
1 seedless cucumber, cut into sticks
1 each red, yellow and orange peppers,
   cut into strips
1 cup green beans, stem ends snipped and boiled
   to crisp-tender

1 **To make dip:** Combine the basil, parsley, garlic, scallions and sour cream in a blender. Blend until creamy, scraping down sides. Pour mixture into a bowl. Whisk in the mayonnaise and season with salt and pepper. Tint a brighter green with food coloring if desired. (Can cover and refrigerate overnight.)

2 **To assemble:** Arrange the vegetables in a serving bowl so they stand up. Cover with moist paper towels and refrigerate until ready to serve with dip.

Getting kids to eat healthier isn't such a nightmare with these Crude-ités with Green Slime Dip (only you will know it's an array of veggies with an herb and onion dip). And you can wave good-bye to the Tortilla Hands (baked red pepper and spinach tortillas, shaped with cookie cutters) since they come with a bowl of salsa for dipping.

Tortilla Hands and Salsa

MAKES: About 24
PREP: 15 min
BAKE: 15–20 min

1 pkg (8 oz) 8-in. red pepper flour tortillas
1 pkg (8 oz) 8-in. spinach flour tortillas
2 Tbsp vegetable oil
1 jar (16 oz) salsa

1 Preheat oven to 375°F. Have baking sheets ready.

2 Brush the tortillas on both sides with the vegetable oil. Using a 3-in. hand-shaped metal cookie cutter, cut as many hand shapes as you can from the tortillas.

3 Arrange the hands on pans in a single layer. Place pans in the oven on separate racks, one above the other. Bake 10 minutes, then remove pans from oven and turn hands over. Switch pans from one rack to the other and bake another 5 to 10 minutes, until light golden and crisp. Transfer to a wire rack to cool completely.

4 Serve hands with salsa.

Ghoulash Stew

SERVES: 8
PREP: 15 min
BAKE: 2½ hr

- 2½ lb beef chuck for stew meat, cut into 1½-in. pieces
- 1 Tbsp flour
- 2 tsp ground cumin
- 1 tsp salt
- ½ tsp ground pepper
- 3 Tbsp vegetable oil
- 1 large onion, chopped
- 1 container (8 oz) sliced mushrooms
- 2 cloves garlic, minced
- 1 cup red wine (optional, substitute broth or water)
- 1 can (16 oz) whole tomatoes in juice, chopped, juices reserved
- 1 container (8 oz) sour cream

1 Preheat oven to 350°F. Toss beef with flour, cumin, salt and pepper. Heat 2 Tbsp of the oil in a large Dutch oven over medium-high heat. Working in batches, brown the meat on all sides. Transfer with a slotted spoon to a bowl.

2 Heat the remaining tablespoon oil in pot. Add the onions, mushrooms and garlic. Cook, stirring, until onions are translucent and mushrooms are golden, about 3 minutes. Add the wine, tomatoes and their juices and bring to a boil. Cover pot and place in the oven. Bake until beef is tender, about 2 to 2½ hours. Skim any excess fat from the top of the stew. Season with salt and pepper if desired.

3 Spoon into bowls. Spoon sour cream into a ziptop bag. Snip a corner from the bag and squeeze a spiral on top of the stew. Draw a toothpick through the sour cream to create a spiderweb. Serve with Cheesy Spiders (for recipe, turn to page 102).

Pomegranate juice adds ghoulish appeal to a Witch's Potion made with lemonade and lemon-lime soda; a dribble of red decorating gel supplies the "gore." It's served from a pitcher so guests can slither on over and refill at will.

Witch's Potion

MAKES: 8 cups
PREP: 10 min

- 8 cups ice
- 1 bottle (1 liter) lemon-lime soda
- 1 qt lemonade
- 1 cup pomegranate juice
- 2 tubes red decorating gel

1 Place the ice cubes in a large pitcher or glasses. Add the soda and lemonade and stir to blend.

2 Gently add the pomegranate juice at the top of the pitcher or glasses to keep the color concentrated.

3 Squeeze some of the gel on the lip of the glasses and pitcher.

Cheesy Spiders

MAKES: 24
PREP: 10 min

1 pkg (8 oz) cream cheese, softened
Black paste food coloring
1 pkg (16 oz) shredded four-cheese mixture
1 pkg (3.5 oz) round rice crunch crackers
    (or 24 of any round cracker)
1 cup chow mein noodles

1 Mix 2 Tbsp of the softened cream cheese with the food coloring to make black. Spoon into a ziptop bag; set aside.

2 Beat the remaining cream cheese with all but 1 cup of the shredded cheese until blended. Shape mixture into 1¼-in. balls.

3 Place the remaining cheese in a shallow bowl. Roll the balls in the cheese to coat. Place one ball on a cracker. Insert 8 chow mein noodles into each ball as the legs of the spider. Snip a very small corner from the bag with the black cream cheese. Pipe eyes on each spider.

4 Serve with stew. Spiders can be made in advance. (Do not put on crackers until ready to serve.) Cover with plastic wrap and store in the refrigerator overnight.

These Cheesy Spiders with their chow mein noodle legs are great finger food, or a melty-crunchy garnish to drop into bubbling bowls of stew (for recipe, turn to page 101).

Truffles

(Bats, Pumpkins, Mummies, Frankenstein)

MAKES: 32
PREP: 45 min
COOK: 5 min
CHILL: about 4 hr

TRUFFLES

¾ cup heavy cream
10 oz semisweet chocolate, chopped
4 Tbsp unsalted butter, softened

DIPPING MIXTURE

½ cup unsweetened cocoa powder
Chocolate wafer cookies, cut into wing shapes
    with a serrated knife
6 oz each white, light green and orange chocolate
    melting wafers
½ cup semisweet chocolate chips
½ cup green chocolate melting wafers
2 Tbsp yellow chocolate melting wafers
2 Tbsp red chocolate melting wafers

TRUFFLES

1 Bring the cream to a boil over medium heat in a medium saucepan. Remove from heat and add the chocolate and butter. Cover and let stand for 5 minutes. Uncover and stir until smooth. Transfer to a medium bowl and refrigerate until firm, about 3 hours.

2 Shape truffle mixture into 32 1-in. balls using a small ice cream scoop or spoon. Place balls on a wax paper-lined baking sheet and freeze until very hard.

DIPPING MIXTURE

1 Line two baking sheets with wax paper.

2 Roll eight of the truffles in cocoa powder to coat. Press two of the chocolate cookie wafer pieces into each truffle as wings.

3 Melt white, light green and orange chocolate melting wafers in separate medium bowls one at a time in the microwave until smooth, about 1 to 2 minutes. Coat eight of the remaining truffles in white chocolate, eight with the light green and eight with the orange to cover, removing any excess chocolate. Transfer truffles to the prepared pans.

4 Melt chips and the remaining chocolate melting wafers in separate bowls and spoon each color into a ziptop bag. Drizzle white chocolate over the white truffles for the mummies. Pipe semisweet chocolate dots for the eyes and dust lightly with cocoa powder.

5 Pipe Frankenstein face on the green truffles with the semisweet, green and red chocolates. Pipe yellow eyes and white fangs for the bats. Pipe semisweet chocolate and green chocolate for the jack-o'-lantern face.

Truffles turn spooky when they're covered in different colors of melting chocolate and cocoa powder, then decorated with piped-on frosting to create bats, pumpkins, mummies and Frankenstein faces.

Haunted Cookie House

MAKES: 1
PREP: Can be made in an afternoon
BAKE: 15–20 min (per batch)

2 cups flour
1 cup unsweetened cocoa powder
4 tsp cinnamon
4 rolls (18 oz each) refrigerated sugar cookie dough
2 boxes (16 oz each) confectioners' sugar
6 Tbsp egg white powder
Brown, purple and orange food coloring
5 brown flat-bottomed ice cream cones
   (Joy brand color cups 2.625 oz.)
2 chocolate ice cream cones
2 bags Hershey's Hugs
1 bag (10 oz) chocolate chips
Decorated cookies (see recipe page 111)
2 cups ground chocolate cookies
Assorted candy pumpkins, candies and cookies
Hot-glue gun (optional, if house is only for
   decoration)

1 Preheat oven to 350°F. Knead the flour, cocoa and cinnamon into the cookie dough, working in batches if necessary, until combined and smooth.

2 Divide dough into quarters and roll out on a lightly floured sheet of parchment paper or foil. Cut out pattern pieces, opposite (see *How to Enlarge Patterns*, page 128), about 2 in. apart. Cut out windows and doors. Leave the house pieces on the paper or foil and transfer to baking sheets.

3 Bake until golden and firm to the touch, 15 to 20 minutes depending on the size of the pieces. Transfer to a wire rack and cool completely. Repeat with the remaining dough and pattern.

4 Meanwhile, beat the confectioners' sugar, egg white powder and ¾ cup water in a large bowl with an electric mixer until thick and smooth.

5 Transfer 1 cup of the frosting to a ziptop bag. Tint 2 cups of the frosting brown and spoon into a ziptop bag. Tint ½ cup orange and 1½ cups purple. Spoon each color into a separate ziptop bag and set aside. Cover the remaining frosting well with a moist paper towel and plastic wrap. (This will be used for the assembly.)

6 Snip a small corner from bag with the purple, white and orange frosting. Pipe around windows and doors on sides of house. Let dry about 1 hour.

7 To assemble (for a quick nonedible centerpiece, follow piece assembly and use a glue gun instead of frosting): Pipe generous lines of white frosting on vertical sides of piece A, B, C and D (large house), and stick sides together. Use cans to support all sides, inside and out. Let dry about 1 hour. Pipe generous lines on vertical sides of pieces E, F, G and H (second story) and attach using cans to support. Let dry at least 1 hour.

8 Attach the roof pieces I and J to the large house with the frosting and let dry about 1 hour. Support the roof with a box or cans. Pipe lines along small roof edge and add pieces K and L. Let dry about 1 hour. Pipe decorative lines on the outside of both stories with the purple frosting. Pipe bone decoration with the white frosting along the sides of the second story.

9 Use a serrated knife to trim 1½ in. from bottom of two of the brown cones. Stack the remaining

three brown cones and add one trimmed cone on top. Place one of the chocolate cones on top of that to create the tower next to the house. Secure tower with some purple frosting.

10 Trim the remaining brown cone to fit on top of the second-story roof. Cut a V shape on either side of cone with a serrated knife. Attach cone to the small roof with some of the brown frosting.

11 Place the larger house on a serving platter. Pipe a generous line of brown frosting along bottom edge of second story. Place on top of larger house and press slightly to secure.

12 Spread a 2-in.-wide band of brown frosting

along bottom roof edge I. Add the unwrapped Hugs as close as possible in rows. Repeat, adding more frosting and Hugs, trimming candy if necessary. Repeat with roof piece J.

13 Spread the brown frosting on roof piece K. Arrange the swirled chips to cover roof, starting at the bottom edge. Repeat with roof piece L.

14 Attach one or two of the decorated cookies to the house if desired using some of the remaining frosting. Hold the cookie for several minutes to make sure that it sets.

15 Spread chocolate cookie crumbs and other decorated cookies and candy pumpkins around house.

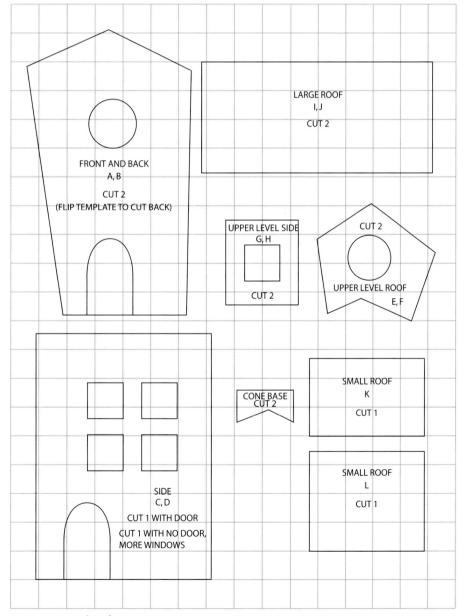

one square = 1 inch

It takes the very best kind of
TLC to build this wickedly wacky
Haunted Cookie House, topped
with frosted roof tiles and peanut-
bar chimneys. A little licorice,
some orange malted milk balls,
and a lot of imagination make this
dessert a spectacular showpiece.

Haunted Cookie House

MAKES: 1
PREP: Can be made in an afternoon

2 cups all-purpose flour
1 cup unsweetened cocoa powder
4 tsp cinnamon
4 rolls (18 oz each) refrigerated sugar cookie dough
2 boxes (16 oz each) confectioners' sugar
6 Tbsp egg-white powder
Orange food coloring

ASSORTED CANDIES AND CRACKERS

Cheese-flavored crackers (about 3 cups)
Candy corn (about 2 cups)
Purple licorice (1 lb pkg), trimmed to 6-in. lengths
Peanut-covered caramel-nougat bars (2 pieces)
Black licorice drops (about 7 pieces)
Orange malted milk balls or jaw breakers (6 pieces)
2 cups ground chocolate wafers
Candy pumpkins (about 1 cup)
Harvest corn
Hot-glue gun (if house is only for decoration)

1 Preheat oven to 350°F. Knead the flour, cocoa and cinnamon into the cookie dough, working in batches if necessary, until combined and smooth.

2 Divide dough into quarters and roll out on a lightly floured sheet of parchment paper or foil. Cut out pattern pieces, right, about 2 in. apart. (See *How to Enlarge Patterns*, page 128.) Cut out windows and doors. Leave the pieces on paper or foil; transfer to baking sheets.

3 Bake until golden and firm to the touch, 15 to 20 minutes depending on the size of the pieces. Transfer to a wire rack and cool completely. Repeat with the remaining dough and pattern. With any of the scraps roll out and cut into tombstones and stepping stones to place around the house.

4 Meanwhile beat the confectioners' sugar and egg-white powder with ¾ cup water in a large bowl with an electric mixer until thick and smooth.

5 Transfer 1 cup of the frosting to a ziptop bag. Cover the remaining frosting well with a moist paper towel and plastic wrap. Snip a small corner from bag and pipe around windows, doors and any other decorations on sides of house. Attach the small candies before frosting sets. Let dry about 1 hour.

6 To assemble, tint all but 1 cup of the remaining frosting bright orange. Spoon some of the orange frosting into a pastry bag fitted with a small star tip. Keep remaining frosting covered. (For quick assembly, but a nonedible centerpiece, follow directions and use a hot-glue gun instead of frosting.)

7 Pipe a line of orange frosting on vertical sides of piece A, B and C and stick sides together. Use cans to support sides. Let dry about 30 minutes. Pipe lines on vertical lines of pieces D, E, and F, using cans to support. Let dry at least 1 hour.

8 Attach the small piece G and roof piece H. Support roof with a can. Pipe lines along roof edge and add pieces I and J. Let dry 30 minutes. Add the remaining roof pieces K and L, and let dry 30 minutes longer. Pipe decorative lines on the outside of the house with the orange frosting.

9 Spread a 2-in.-wide band of orange frosting along bottom roof edge of pieces J and K. Add the crackers, overlapping the rows. Repeat adding more frosting and crackers, trimming crackers if necessary.

10 Spread the orange frosting on roof piece H. Arrange the candy corn starting at the bottom edge.

11 Spread the white frosting on the remaining roof and add the purple licorice, trimming if necessary.

12 Trim and add the peanut candy bar as the chimneys, add the black licorice dots and orange malted milk balls. Spread the chocolate cookie crumbs around house. Add the tombstones, steps and pumpkins. Let dry at least 1 hour.

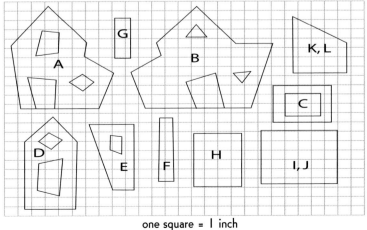

one square = 1 inch

Chocolate Apple Cat Faces

MAKES: 4
PREP: 25 min

4 Granny Smith apples
Wooden sticks
1 bag (12 oz) semisweet chocolate chips
1 Tbsp solid vegetable shortening
1 cup chocolate jimmies (sprinkles)
8 yellow banana-shaped candies (Runts)
4 pink heart-shaped candies (Runts)
1 chocolate wafer cookie, cut into eighths
   with a serrated knife
1 tube each pink and white decorating frosting

1 Wash and dry the apples. Insert the wooden sticks into the tops of each apple. Line a baking pan with wax paper.

2 Melt the chips and the shortening on low heat in a saucepan. Stir constantly until completely melted.

3 Put chocolate jimmies into a medium bowl. Working with one apple at a time, dip apple into the melted chocolate to cover completely. Allow excess to drip off. Coat apple in chocolate jimmies and place on prepared baking pan. Place pan into refrigerator. Chill until chocolate is set.

4 Spoon the remaining chocolate into a ziptop bag. Snip a small corner from the bag and use chocolate to attach the chocolate wafer pieces as ears. Pipe the eyes, nose and mouth and add the candies. Pipe the pink frosting for the ears and the white frosting as the whiskers.

Candy Apples with Gummy Worms

MAKES: 4
PREP: 25 min
COOK: about 10 min

4 Granny Smith apples
Wooden sticks
¾ cup praline crunch ice cream topping
1 cup sugar
½ cup water
Pinch cream of tartar
Green food coloring
4 gummy worms

1 Wash and dry the apples. Insert the wooden sticks into the top of the apples. Line a baking pan with foil. Sprinkle ½ cup of the praline crunch topping over the foil.

2 Combine the sugar, water and cream of tartar in a medium saucepan. Bring to a boil, cover and boil for 3 minutes. Uncover and cook until a candy thermometer reaches 300°F or hard-crack stage, approximately 3 minutes. Remove pan from stove and place in a bowl of hot water. Tint green if desired with a few drops of food coloring.

3 Dip apples, one at a time, into the candy to coat. Allow excess candy to drip off. Place apple on prepared pan. Sprinkle top with some of the remaining praline crunch. Add the gummy worm. Continue with the remaining apples and ingredients. Let apples cool completely before peeling from the foil.

These smiling candy-garnished Chocolate Apple Cat Faces, left, and green praline-crunch-dusted Candy Apples with Gummy Worms, opposite, make fresh fruit ever so enticing.

Decorated Cookies

(Devil, Frankenstein, Webs, Bats, Candy Corn, Tombstones, Pumpkins, Coffins, Cauldron, Skeleton, Ghosts, Witch Hat, Witch Boot, Black Cat)

MAKES: 42
PREP: Depends on skill level
BAKE: 10–12 min per batch
DRYING: 1 hr

2 rolls (18 oz each) refrigerated sugar
    cookie dough
1 ⅓ cups flour
2 recipes Royal Frosting (recipe follows)
Orange, yellow, gray, brown, black, purple, light
    green and red food paste coloring
Black, brown, red, green, white and orange
    decorating sugars (optional)

1 Preheat oven to 350°F. Coat four baking sheets with cooking spray.

2 Knead the cookie dough with the flour on a clean work surface until smooth.

3 Divide dough into quarters. Working with one piece at a time (keep remaining dough refrigerated) roll out dough on a lightly floured work surface to a scant ¼-in. thickness. Cut out as many shapes as possible with the cookie cutters. Transfer shapes with an offset spatula to prepared pans. Roll up the scraps.

4 Bake until cookies are golden around edges, about 10 to 12 minutes. Transfer to a wire rack and cool completely. Repeat with remaining dough.

5 Divide the Royal Frosting into nine bowls. Using food paste coloring, tint each portion a different color, leaving one white. Keep the bowls covered with plastic wrap to prevent frosting from drying. Spoon half of each color into a small ziptop bag. Thin remaining half of each color with 1 tsp of water until it has the texture of slightly whipped cream. Spoon each color into separate ziptop bags.

6 Snip a very small corner from the bags with the thicker frosting. Pipe outlines of designs on cookies as shown. Snip a very small corner from bags of thinned frosting and fill in outlined areas. Allow cookies to dry for at least an hour. (If you don't, the colors piped on top will bleed into the lighter colors.)

7 Pipe details on top of dry cookies with thick frosting. Sprinkle with colored sugars while still wet, if desired.

Royal Frosting

MAKES: About 4 cups

2 boxes (16 oz each) confectioners' sugar
6 Tbsp egg white powder or meringue powder
¾ cup water, plus more for thinning

1 Combine the confectioners' sugar, egg white powder and water in a large bowl. Beat with an electric mixture until thick and fluffy, about 1 minute.

2 Use immediately or transfer to an airtight container and store in the refrigerator for up to 1 week. Stir well before using.

Spiderwebs, Tombstones, Pumpkins, Frankenstein, Devils, Bats, Coffins, Witch Hats and Boot, Black Cats, Skulls and more—they'll all disappear in a flash when you set out a platter of these devilishly Decorated Cookies. Start with refrigerated cookie dough, then let your imagination fly with frosting and colored sugar.

Your favorite cupcake mix or recipe is easily transformed into a Wicked Witch, a One-Eyed Monster, a Debonair Devil and a Flying Crow. Just add colored frosting, miniature candies, crisp cookies, ice cream cones, licorice laces and decorating sugar for details.

Wicked Witch

MAKES: 12
PREP: 30 min

- 2 cans (16 oz each) vanilla frosting
- Yellow, red, brown, green, orange, and purple paste food coloring
- 12 baked and cooled cupcakes
- 2 each green, orange and purple gumdrop candies, cut in half lengthwise
- 24 brown mini-M&M's
- 12 ropes Twisted Berry Twizzlers
- 24 chocolate wafer cookies
- 12 chocolate ice cream cones

1 Tint 9 Tbsp of the frosting yellow and spoon into a ziptop bag. Tint 6 Tbsp frosting red and 6 Tbsp brown. Divide up the remaining frosting and tint it green, orange and purple. Spoon each color into a ziptop bag.

2 Spread the green, orange and purple frosting on top of the cupcakes to cover. Spoon any remaining frosting into a ziptop bag. Insert a cut gumdrop as a nose. Add the M&M's for the eyes.

3 Snip a small corner from the bags with the frosting. Pipe a squiggle mouth with the red frosting. Pipe brown frosting as the eyebrows and a dot of frosting for the wart.

4 Cut several of the Twizzlers into 1-in. pieces for the bangs and 3-in. pieces for hair. Press the bangs and longer pieces on sides of the cupcakes.

5 Place the cupcakes on their sides on chocolate wafers.

6 Use a serrated knife to trim about 1 in. from the wide end of each cone. Attach the cone to the chocolate wafer with the yellow frosting. Place hat on top of the cupcake and secure with some frosting if necessary.

One-Eyed Monster Cupcake

MAKES: 12
PREP: 30 min

- 1 can (16 oz) vanilla frosting
- Green, red and yellow food coloring
- 12 baked and cooled cupcakes
- ½ cup each light green and red decorating sugar
- Red licorice laces
- 12 Mega M&M's
- Black licorice laces, cut into 1-in. pieces
- 1 tube black decorating frosting

1 Spoon ¾ cup of the frosting into a ziptop bag. Divide the remaining frosting and tint it light green with the green and yellow food coloring and orange with the red and yellow. Frost tops of cupcakes. Roll cupcake edges in the green and red decorating sugar as shown. (You can make the monsters other colors, too.)

2 Cut the red licorice into twelve 2½-in. pieces and twenty-four ¼-in. pieces. Attach as the mouth on the lower half of the cupcakes. Snip a small corner from bag with the frosting and pipe teeth along the lower part of mouth.

3 Snip a large corner from ziptop bag and pipe a large dot of vanilla frosting for the eye. Add the M&M's as the iris. Insert three to four pieces of black licorice laces as the lashes. Pipe the pupil with the black frosting on top of the candy eye.

Debonair Devil

MAKES: 12
PREP: 30 min

   1 can (16 oz) vanilla frosting
   Red paste food coloring
   12 baked and cooled cupcakes
   1 cup red sprinkles
   12 red M&M's
   24 brown mini-M&M's
   6 red spice drops
   3 chocolate wafer cookies
   12 red heart candy decorations
   1 tube brown or black decorating frosting

1 Tint frosting bright red with the food coloring. Frost tops of cupcakes with the red frosting. Roll edges in red sprinkles.

2 Place red M&M's sideways, in center of cupcake as the nose. Add the brown M&M's as the eyes. Cut the spice drops into quarters and attach at the top of the cupcakes as the horns.

3 Cut each chocolate wafer with a serrated knife into four ¾-in. triangles. Attach wafer as the beard on the cupcake. Add the heart candies as the mouth. Pipe mustache and eyebrows with the tube frosting.

Flying Crow

MAKES: 12
PREP: 30 min

   1 can (16 oz) vanilla frosting
   Yellow food coloring
   12 baked and cooled cupcakes
   1 cup yellow crystal decorating sugar
   1 can (16 oz) dark-chocolate frosting
   12 chocolate wafer cookies
   12 yellow banana-shaped candies (Runts)
   12 red candy decors

1 Tint the vanilla frosting bright yellow. Spread the yellow frosting on top of the cupcakes and make smooth. Roll the edge in the decorating sugar.

2 Spoon some of the chocolate frosting into a ziptop bag. Snip a ¼-in. corner from the bag and pipe a large dot of frosting on one side of the cupcake as the head. Pipe another dot of frosting next to the first, in the center, as the body.

3 Using a serrated knife, gently cut two ½-in.-wide wing shapes, as shown, from each of the chocolate wafers. Trim the remaining pieces into 1-in. triangle tails.

4 Insert the wafer pieces into the cupcake as the wings and tail. Press the banana candy into the chocolate frosting as the beak. Add the red candy decor as the eye; pipe on dark chocolate for legs.

Silly Spider

MAKES: 12
PREP: 30 min

    1 can (16 oz) chocolate frosting
    12 baked and cooled cupcakes
    1 cup chocolate sprinkles
    12 mini-chocolate sandwich cookies
    12 (1 pkg) 2-foot-long red licorice laces
    3 rolls red fruit leather, each cut into eight
        1-in. diamonds
    1 tube *each* red and white decorating frosting

1 Spread 2½ Tbsp of chocolate frosting over the top of each cupcake. Roll tops in the chocolate sprinkles to cover completely.

2 Spoon the remaining chocolate frosting into a ziptop bag. Snip a small corner from the bag and pipe a dollop of frosting on one side of each cupcake; attach the chocolate cookie.

3 Use a toothpick to make eight holes along edge for the legs as shown. Cut the red licorice into 3-in.-long pieces and insert one piece into each hole as legs.

4 Attach the fruit leather diamonds on top of cupcakes with some of the frosting. Pipe a red mouth and white eyes and nose with the decorating frosting. Pipe the eyes with the remaining chocolate frosting.

Scare the cobwebs out into the open with these Broom Cookies, crafted from cookie dough and red frosting, then shaped with the tines of a fork and topped with a pretzel-rod handle.

Broom Cookies

MAKES: 36
PREP: 35 min
BAKE: 12–15 min

    1 bag (17.5 oz) peanut butter cookie mix
    ⅓ cup flour
    1 bag (9 oz) 12 honey-wheat multigrain
        pretzel sticks
    1 tube red decorating frosting

1 Preheat oven to 375°F. Coat two baking sheets with nonstick spray; set aside. Prepare cookie mix according to package directions with the addition of the flour. Mix until smooth.

2 Divide dough into 36 pieces. Shape the dough pieces into triangles about ¼ in. thick. Arrange pieces about 2 in. apart on baking sheets. Insert the pretzel stick into one corner, ½ in. into the dough.

3 Press the tines of a fork into the dough to make the broom bristles.

4 Bake 12 to 15 minutes until golden and cookies are slightly firm. Transfer to a wire rack and cool completely.

5 When cookies are cool, pipe a line of red frosting on the top of the bristles.

Wicked Witch

MAKES: 24
PREP: 1 hr

- 2 cans (16 oz each) whipped vanilla frosting
- Violet food coloring
- 2 boxes chocolate ice cream cones
- 24 chocolate wafer cookies
- 1 tube each yellow, black, white and orange decorating frosting
- 24 baked and cooled cupcakes made from your favorite cake mix, without liners
- 24 chocolate sugar cookies
- 2 boxes (4.8 oz each) watermelon streamers or green licorice laces
- 6 purple spice drops

1 Spoon ¼ cup of the frosting into a ziptop bag; set aside. Tint the remaining frosting light violet.

2 Gently trim 1 inch from open end of cones with a serrated knife. Attach the open end to the chocolate wafer cookie with the yellow tube frosting; set aside.

3 Place the cupcakes, small end up on the chocolate sugar cookies. Cover completely with the violet frosting. Pull apart and add the watermelon streamers or licorice as the hair and bangs.

4 Cut the spice drops into quarters and shape into a witch nose. Press the spice drop into the cupcake as the nose. Pipe the eyes, pupils, eye brows, warts and mouth with the colored frosting, referring to photo. Place the cones on top for hats.

Shrieking Ghosts

MAKES: 24
PREP: 30 min
DRYING: 24 hr

- 3 to 4 Tbsp cornstarch
- 12 oz (half a 24-oz box) premade white rolled fondant
- 1 can (16 oz) vanilla frosting
- Orange food coloring
- 24 baked and cooled cupcakes in liners prepared from your favorite cake mix
- ½ cup orange decorating sugar

1 Lightly dust a work surface with some of the cornstarch. Working with a quarter of the fondant at a time, roll out fondant to a generous ⅛-in. thickness. Add more cornstarch when necessary to prevent sticking. Use a 3- to 4-in. ghost-shaped cookie cutter to cut out shapes and transfer them to a baking sheet. Cut out eyes and mouth with the round tip of a pastry tip or a small straw. Let ghosts dry for at least 24 hours before assembly.

2 Tint frosting bright orange with food coloring. Spread tops of the cupcakes with the orange frosting, making a swirl on top. Roll the edges in the orange decorating sugar. Press ghosts into the cupcakes.

NOTE: Ghosts can be made up to 1 week in advance. Once dry, layer on baking sheets with wax paper between the layers. Tightly wrap baking sheets with plastic wrap.

Mummy

MAKES: 24
PREP: 30 min

3 to 4 Tbsp cornstarch
1 box (24 oz) premade fondant
1 can (16 oz) vanilla frosting
24 baked and cooled cupcakes in liners prepared from your favorite cake mix
24 mini-red gummy fish or red gum drops

1 Lightly dust a work surface with some of the cornstarch. Working with a quarter of the fondant at a time, roll out fondant to a ⅛-in. thickness. To prevent sticking, add more cornstarch when necessary. Use a pastry wheel to cut strips, about ½ to ¾ in. wide and 4 in. long (the pieces can be uneven). Transfer pieces to a baking pan and cover with plastic wrap.

2 Spoon 2 Tbsp of the frosting into a ziptop bag; set aside. Spread tops of cupcakes with the remaining frosting. Cut the gummy fish in half lengthwise. Cut one half into small pieces for the eyes and use the other half for a mouth shape. Attach candies with the reserved frosting in ziptop bag.

3 Overlap the fondant strips over cupcake tops to look like bandages. Trim the overhang with scissors.

Sorcerer's Hat

MAKES: 24
PREP: 30 min

72 chocolate Tootsie Roll Midgies
24 chocolate-covered round cookies
1 tube blue decorating frosting
Silver dragees
24 baked and cooled cupcakes in liners prepared from your favorite cake mix
1 can (16 oz) vanilla frosting
Blue decorating sugar

1 Heat about 12 candies at a time in the microwave for about 2 to 3 seconds until softened. Unwrap and combine 3 candies at a time into a cone shape. Place each cone on top of a chocolate-covered cookie (for brim). Score the side of each hat with a small knife.

2 Pipe blue stars and dots around hat. Add the silver dragees to dots.

3 Spread the tops of the cupcakes with the vanilla frosting. Roll edges in decorating sugar. Place hats on top of cupcakes.

Grinning Skulls

MAKES: 24
PREP: 15 min

1 can (16 oz) vanilla frosting
Yellow food coloring
24 baked and cooled cupcakes in liners prepared from your favorite cake mix
24 premade fondant skulls

1 Tint the frosting yellow. Spread the tops of the cupcakes with the yellow frosting.

2 Press a skull carefully in the center of each cupcake.

Graveyard Plots

MAKES: 24
PREP: 30 min

2 cans (16 oz each) whipped vanilla frosting
6 chocolate candy bars (1.55 oz each)
24 baked and cooled cupcakes in liners prepared
    from your favorite cake mix
Green food coloring
48 premade fondant bones

1 Spoon ¾ cup of the frosting into a pastry bag fitted with a plain #2 tip. Cut the candy bars into quarters along the indentations to make the tombstones. Trim each top with a small knife to make either a rounded or angled tombstone. Pipe decorations on the flat side of chocolates for tombstone epitaphs.

2 Cut a small slit into the top of each cupcake and insert a chocolate tombstone (it is fine if it goes in at an angle).

3 Tint the remaining frosting green and spoon it into a ziptop bag. Snip a small corner from the bag and pipe grass all over the top of the cupcake. Insert the bones or lay them on top.

Black Cats

MAKES: 8 to 10
PREP: 30 min
COOL: 1 hr
STAND: 1 hr

1 bag (10 oz) marshmallows
3 Tbsp butter or margarine
6 cups cocoa-flavored rice cereal
1 can (16 oz) dark chocolate frosting
1 tube white decorating icing
Small round red candies

1 Spray a 10½ x 15½-in. rimmed baking pan with cooking spray. Melt the marshmallows and butter in a large saucepan over medium heat, stirring frequently. When smooth stir in the rice cereal, tossing to coat evenly. Grease hands and press cereal mixture into prepared pan. Let cool at least 1 hour.

2 Using a cookie cutter or template and paring knife, cut out cat shapes. Transfer cats to a wire rack placed over a baking sheet.

3 Heat chocolate frosting in the microwave until pourable, about 5 seconds. Pour the frosting over the cats to coat evenly. Make two white dabs of icing for eyes and add red candies for pupils. Let cats set about 1 hour.

Turn mozzarella, blue corn chips and salsa into a crunchy, delicious Dracula Appetizer that will have your guests biting in with relish.

Dracula Appetizer

MAKES: About 36
PREP: 25 min

1 bag blue tortilla chips
1 container (12 oz) small fresh mozzarella balls, halved
1 can (6 oz) jumbo pitted black olives, drained
1 small red pepper

SALSA

1 jar (12 oz) medium salsa
½ cup drained roasted red peppers, chopped
¼ cup chopped chives
1 clove garlic, minced
Salt and freshly ground black pepper

1 Arrange the whole blue tortilla chips on serving platter or platters, reserving the broken pieces for another use. Place a mozzarella half, cut side down, on longest corner.

2 Cut the black olives into ¾-in. triangles and place on top of mozzarella balls as hair. Cut 2 small dots as the eyes with the olive scraps. Use one of the mozzarella balls and cut into small pieces for the nose. Cut the red pepper into small triangles as the fangs.

3 Salsa: Mix all of the ingredients together in a small bowl. Season to taste with salt and pepper. Serve salsa with the chips.

Bats

MAKES: 24
PREP: 30 min
BAKE: 15 min

1 pkg (17.3 oz) frozen puff pastry sheets
1 large egg, lightly beaten
¼ cup poppy seeds
1 lb combination of sliced ham, cheese, turkey
    or other deli selections
Mayonnaise and mustard

1 Thaw puff pastry according to package directions. Preheat the oven to 400°F. Line two baking pans with parchment paper.

2 Roll out one sheet of the puff pastry on a lightly floured surface to make smooth. Brush the top lightly with the beaten egg. Sprinkle the top with half of the poppy seeds. Cut into 3- to 4-in. bat shapes with a cookie cutter and transfer to the prepared pans. Repeat with the remaining dough.

3 Bake 10 to 15 minutes or until bats are puffed and golden brown. Transfer to a wire rack to cool.

4 Cut out deli meats and cheeses with the same cookie cutter. Spoon about 1 Tbsp mayonnaise into a ziptop bag.

5 Cut the bats in half horizontally. Spread with mayonnaise or mustard and fill with desired deli selections. Top with poppy seed side. Snip a small corner of bag with mayonnaise and pipe dots as eyes on top.

Puff pastry, biscuit dough, cheese, cold cuts and mini-dogs make it easy for these tasty Bats and Moths to fly right onto your Halloween buffet table. Don't forget the mayo and mustard!

Moths

MAKES: 30
PREP: 30 min
BAKE: 16 min

2 tubes (16.3 oz each) refrigerated biscuit dough
12 mini-hot dogs, halved lengthwise
2 Tbsp poppy seeds
Thin pretzel sticks
Mustard

1 Preheat oven to 375°F. Line a baking sheet with foil. Unmold refrigerated biscuits. Flatten each biscuit slightly and cut out desired shape. (Small moth about 2½ inches wing to wing, or use a 3-in. butterfly cookie cutter for larger size.) Transfer shapes to the prepared cookie sheet.

2 For smaller moths, place the hot dog half onto the smaller shapes as the body and sprinkle the wings with the poppy seeds. For larger moths, simply sprinkle the butterfly shapes with poppy seeds.

3 Bake until puffed and golden brown; 12 to 16 minutes. Transfer to a wire rack to cool. Insert pretzel sticks as antennae in the larger moths. Serve with mustard.

Eyeballs

MAKES: 36
PREP: 45 min
CHILL: 2 hr

1 cup creamy peanut butter
½ cup unsalted butter, softened
2 to 2½ cups confectioners' sugar
1 bag (12 oz) white chocolate chips
2 Tbsp solid vegetable shortening
1 tube each red, white and green decorating frosting
36 brown M&M's

1 Stir the peanut butter and butter in a medium bowl until smooth. Gradually add the confectioners' sugar until thick and smooth and well combined. (The mixture should be thick and easy to roll into balls.)

2 Line a baking sheet with wax paper. Shape mixture into 36 1-in. balls. Place balls on prepared baking sheet and refrigerate about 1 hour or until firm.

3 Meanwhile melt the white chocolate with the vegetable shortening over a double boiler until smooth. Carefully drop chilled peanut butter balls into the chocolate to coat, and scoop them out with a fork, letting excess drip off through the tines (be careful not to stick the balls). Return balls to wax paper-lined baking sheet; refrigerate until set.

4 Squeeze frostings into separate ziptop bags. Snip a very small corner from each bag. Pipe red frosting lines from center out for the veins. Pipe a dot of green frosting on top. Place the M&M's in the center and pipe a white line on one side. Keep refrigerated until ready to serve.

Harmless kid-party favorites—salsa and chips, mini-hot dogs, Bloody (Fruit) Punch, sandwiches and cookies—change into eerie shapes to transform your Halloween party into a celebration of scary fun.

Do guests dare to grab juicy Eyeballs made of creamy peanut butter, sugar, M&M's and frosting? We're willing to bet these will disappear so fast, you won't believe your eyes!

Bloody (Fruit) Punch

MAKES: 1 gallon
PREP: 10 min

4 tubes red decorating gel
1 qt pomegranate juice, chilled
1 qt cranberry juice, chilled
2 qt lemon/lime soda, chilled

1 Squeeze the red gel around rims and down the sides of glasses and pitcher.

2 Pour the juices and soda into the serving pitcher; stir. Add ice if desired.

Cookie Pops

MAKES: 24
PREP: 20 min
BAKE: 10-12 min per batch

1 ⅓ cups all-purpose flour
2 rolls (18 oz each) refrigerated sugar
  cookie dough
24 lollipop sticks
1 recipe Royal Frosting (see recipe page 111)
Orange, black, green and purple paste food coloring
Green candy-coated chocolates and sliced almonds
  (for flies on web cookies)
White and black decorating sugar

1 Preheat oven to 350°F. Knead the flour into the sugar cookie dough until smooth. Roll out the dough on a lightly floured surface to a ¼-in. thickness.

2 Cut out desired shapes with cookie cutters and transfer to baking sheets, placing them about 2 in. apart. Insert the lollipop stick ¾ of the way into the cookie. Bake until golden brown, about 10 to 12 minutes. Transfer to a wire rack and cool completely. Repeat with remaining dough.

3 **Royal Frosting:** Divide frosting into five bowls: Tint 1 orange, 1 black, 1 green and 1 purple and leave 1 part white. Spoon half of each color, except green, into a ziptop bag. Thin the remaining frostings in bowls with a small amount of water until the texture of slightly whipped cream. Spoon each color into a ziptop bag.

4 Snip a small corner from the bags with the thicker frosting and pipe outlines of cookies with desired colors. Snip a small corner in bags with thinned frosting. Fill in outlines with thinned frosting. Pipe decorative designs on top and using a toothpick (while frosting is still wet), pull frosting to create patterns. Repeat with remaining cookies and frosting. For web cookie flies, add 1 green candy and 2 almonds for wings.

5 Pipe details and sprinkle with decorating sugars while piped frosting is still wet. Let cookies dry completely, about 3 hours.

Mini-Witch Hats

SKILL LEVEL: Beginner

MATERIALS: Black construction paper; scissors; craft glue; pom-poms in assorted colors; fun foam sheets in assorted colors, including black; pinking shears.

DIRECTIONS:

1　Using regular scissors, cut paper into triangle about 7 inches high. Roll into cone slightly more than 1½ inches across bottom; glue to form top of hat.

2　Trim off tip of cone; glue pompom to tip. Cut 5-in. circle of foam; cut 1½ inches hole in center. Trim edges with pinking shears to form brim of hat.

3　Slip brim down hat (foam will stretch to fit tightly).

4　Cut an additional brim if desired, making it about 4 inches across; slip down hat so it rests on lower brim.

Your guests will want to grab one of these Mini-Witch Hats, which make a fashion statement on top of soda bottles chilling in the ice bucket.

Now That's Cool! A fat and funny faux jack-o'-lantern transforms itself into a festive pumpkin cooler with the addition of a metal bowl and a bagful of ice. Fill with colorful sodas, juice or other libations to quell a monstrous thirst.

Frankenstein Fingers

MAKES: 8
PREP: 20 min

- 1 cup green candy melting wafers
- 8 pretzel rods
- 4 red non-sugared gumdrops (like Dots), halved vertically

1 Line baking sheet with waxed paper. Place candy melting wafers in a glass measuring cup and microwave 1 to 2 minutes until just melted, stirring every 15 seconds. Dip pretzel rods into melted wafers to cover by half. Shake off excess and place on prepared baking sheet.

2 Spoon remaining melted wafers into a resealable food storage bag and snip off small corner. Pipe lines and knuckles on top. Attach cut candies as the nails on tip of pretzel rod. Refrigerate until set, about 5 minutes.

Mummy Digits

MAKES: 8
PREP: 20 min

- 1 cup white chocolate chips
- 8 pretzel rods
- 1 tsp unsweetened cocoa powder

1 Line baking sheet with waxed paper. Place chocolate chips in glass measuring cup and microwave 1 to 2 minutes until just melted, stirring every 15 seconds. Dip pretzel rods into the chocolate to cover by half. Shake off excess and place on prepared baking sheet.

2 Spoon remaining chocolate into a ziptop bag and snip off a small corner. Pipe lines over top as bandages. Refrigerate until set, about 5 minutes. Dust tops with cocoa.

Who knew creature claws could be so yummy? Delectable Frankenstein Fingers, Mummy Digits and Werewolf Claws will have your guests howling for more.

Werewolf Claws

MAKES: 8
PREP: 20 min

- 1 cup milk chocolate chips
- 8 pretzel rods
- ½ cup chocolate sprinkles
- 8 slivered almonds

1 Line baking sheet with waxed paper. Place chocolate chips in glass measuring cup and microwave 1 to 2 minutes until just melted, stirring every 15 seconds. Dip pretzel rods into chocolate to cover by half. Shake off excess and place on prepared baking sheet.

2 Cover pretzels with the sprinkles to cover completely. Place almond at tip for nails. Refrigerate until set, about 5 minutes.

How to Enlarge Patterns

Using a colored pencil and ruler, mark a grid on the pattern by connecting grid lines around the edges. On a sheet of paper, mark a grid of 1-inch squares (or size given), making the same number of squares as on the pattern. To do this, use graph paper with 1-inch squares. In each square, draw the same lines as in the corresponding square on the pattern. Another way to enlarge is by using a photocopier.

Credits

Pages 6, 8-10, 12-13, 22-23, 24 (bottom), 25, 28-29, 30, 33-37, 42-43, 46-49, 78-86, 87 (top), 89: Produced and styled by Dan Pasky, photographs by Erik Rank.

Page 11: photograph by Jeff McNamara.

Pages 14 to 19: Pumpkin designs and carvings by Michael Natiello for Historic Hudson Valley's "The Great Jack O'Lantern Blaze," photographs by Bryan Haeffele for Historic Hudson Valley. Event information at www.hudsonvalley.org.

Page 20: Photograph by Theresa Raffetto.

Pages 24 (top), 26-27, 40-41, 72, 76-77, 87 (bottom), 88: Produced and styled by Amy Leonard and Ingrid Leess, photographs by Aimee Herring.

Pages 31, 68-71, 74-75, 92-93: Produced and styled by Ingrid Leess, photographs by Aimee Herring.

Pages 32, 38-39, 44-45, 90-91: Designed by Robin Tarnoff for Velcro Brand Fabric Fusion, photographs by Deborah Ory.

Pages 50-57: Designed by Karin Lidbeck-Brent, photographs by Erik Rank.

Pages 58, 60, 62, 64, 66: Designed by Karin Lidbeck-Brent, photographs by Aimee Herring.

Pages 59, 61, 63, 65, 67: Designed by Karin Lidbeck-Brent, instructions by Michele Filon, photographs by Aimee Herring.

Pages 94-105, 108-115, 126 (bottom): Produced and styled by Dan Pasky, food styling and recipes by Karen Tack, photographs by Erik Rank.

Pages 106-107, 116-119: Recipes produced by Wendy Kromer, food styling by Karen Tack, prop styling by Karen Quatsoe, photographs by Deborah Ory.

Pages 120-125, 126 (top), 127: Styled by Ingrid Leess, food styling by Karen Tack, photographs by Aimee Herring.